Turning Your World

Right Side Up

Turning Your World

World

Right Side Up

Jim Smoke

PUBLISHING
Colorado Springs, Colorado

TURNING YOUR WORLD RIGHT SIDE UP
Copyright © 1995 by Jim Smoke
All rights reserved. International copyright secured.

Library of Congress Cataloging-in-Publication Data

Smoke, Jim.
    Turning your world right side up : hope and healing for the divorced and widowed / Jim Smoke.
       p. cm.
    Includes bibliographical references.
    ISBN 1-56179-404-X
    1. Single people—United States—Life skills guides.   2. Divorced people—United States—Life
skills guides.   3. Widows—United States—Life skills guides.   4. Widowers—United States—Life skills
guides.   5. Identity (Psychology).   I. Title.
HQ800.4.U6S66   1995
646.7'008'652—dc20   95-19394
                                                            CIP

Published by Focus on the Family Publishing,
Colorado Springs, Colorado 80995.
Distributed in the U.S.A. and Canada by Word Books, Dallas, Texas.

Unless otherwise identified, Scripture quotations are from the Revised Standard Version of the Bible,
copyrights 1946, 1952, 1971, and 1973. Quotations designated KJV are from the King James version of the
Bible.

Scripture quotations identified Phillips are from The New Testament in Modern English (Revised Edition),
translated by J.B. Phillips, © J.B. Phillips 1958, 1960, 1972. Used by permission of Macmillan Publishing
Co., Inc.

Quotation from the poem "Ambivalence" is by Nancy D. Potts, *Beginning Again: The Challenge of the
Formerly Married.*

Quotation from "The 59th Street Bridge Song" ©1966, 1967 Paul Simon. Used by permission.

Diligent effort has been made to secure permission for all quotations used in this book. Some portions of
this book appeared in an earlier book, *Suddenly Single*, by the author.

The author is represented by the literary agency of Alive Communications, P.O. Box 49068, Colorado
Springs, Colorado 80949.

Editor: Deena Davis
Cover design: Candi L. Park
Cover photo: Rich Buzzelli

Printed in the United States of America

95 96 97 98 99/10 9 8 7 6 5 4 3 2 1

To Carol ~
Wife, friend, mother, grandmother,
researcher, cutie, computer whiz
& skilled juggler of life's
responsibility.

Contents

Preface

This book describes a journey well known to millions of "suddenly single" adults. It is a collection of conversations overheard as I have traveled across America. It contains the questions, fears, dreams, frustrations, doubts, and hopes of men and women who are single again because of the death or divorce of their spouses.

This is not a book about the crisis of going through death and divorce. There are many good books that deal with those issues. It is about what happens well after the ink has dried on divorce decrees and death certificates. It is about picking up the pieces and putting life back together. "Is there life after the death or divorce of a spouse?" I would answer with a resounding *Yes!*

Of the 70 million single adults in our country, many are divorced or widowed. Some of their frustrations can be summed up in the words of one lady who stopped me after a singles conference: "I've been divorced for three years. I am well past the crisis. I don't know who I am anymore and even worse, I don't know what I will become."

I hope to honestly, practically, and simply shed some light on statements like this and answer some questions you might have asked yourself after becoming single again.

After 20 years in Single Adult Ministry and speaking at over 700 retreats, seminars, and singles conferences, I have come to realize that the questions are the same. It's only the faces of the men and women asking them that change.

JIM SMOKE
Cypress, California
1995

In Transition
or Out of Commission?

"We need to encounter our life experiences, not ignore them."

Julia Cameron

As I speak to and counsel thousands of single adults each year, one word seems to pop up in every conversation: *transition*. The dictionary defines *transition* as "a passage from one place, condition, or action to another; change."

Suddenly becoming single again after the death of or divorce from a mate brings a person face to face with changes he or she neither planned for nor desired. The plan, in fact, was to live happily ever after, and the wedding ceremony seemed to guarantee it. But there are no guarantees in life!

Becoming single again presents two basic struggles. First, there is the struggle with *loss* and the acceptance and resolution of it. For most people, the initial process of coping with that loss takes two to three years.

The second struggle is about facing the challenges of *rebuilding life* after the loss of a spouse. Rebuilding your life is the struggle we will address in this book.

How Do You Know Where You Are Right Now?

I speak with many single-again people who ask me to help them pinpoint where they are in their struggle and what lies ahead. They want to know, "Am

1

I through the crisis? Am I ready to rebuild?" Some people I meet choose to live at the crossroad of their crisis.

If you think you're ready to rebuild your life but you're not sure, let me suggest several questions to help you evaluate where you are right now.

1. Do you constantly talk about your former spouse?
2. Do you repeatedly tell your divorce or death story?
3. Do you feel sorry for yourself most of the time?
4. Do you often play make-believe games in your mind?
5. Do you blame your former spouse for your present condition?
6. Do you feel life has dealt you a cruel, unfair blow?
7. Do you tend to live more in the past than in the present?

If you answered yes to one or more of these questions, you may still be struggling with your crisis. You cannot begin the rebuilding process as long as you're caught in the crisis.

The Three Stages of Rebuilding

Most people must work through three stages to rebuild their lives as single-again men and women.

The first stage involves looking back on your life and saying, "If only I had . . . " You don't have to think too hard to come up with an immediate list of things you wish you had done differently. But the truth is, you can't change history or memories. You can only learn from them. Looking back with regret dulls your hope for today.

In my work, I often refer to what the Bible tells us about situations we may face. The apostle Paul said, "Forgetting what lies behind and straining forward to what lies ahead, I press on toward the goal for the prize of the upward call of God in Christ Jesus" (Phil. 3:13-14). Paul had experiences in his yesterdays that he wanted to forget. He knew the only way this could happen was to live today with his eyes open toward tomorrow.

Thinking in reverse only prevents you from moving forward. Put all your yesterdays in your file drawer, and concentrate on building today.

A second stage is known as forward-fear projection. It simply means that you look at tomorrow and say, "What if . . . ?" What if you run out of money? What if you never remarry? What if you get sick and have no one to look after you? What if the stock market crashes and the gasoline supply dries up? What if your children become delinquents? The worry list is endless.

Fear of the future can immobilize you in the present and keep you from making plans that will help you rebuild your life. Your future is best handled by placing it in God's hands. Writing to the early Christians at Philippi, Paul said, "Don't worry over anything whatever . . . tell God every detail of your needs in earnest and thankful prayer" (Phil. 4:6, Phillips).

The future can be frightening for everyone, not just for those who are single again. Only God can translate that fear into trust.

The third stage deals with living in the present. At the conclusion of a divorce-recovery workshop, Sara presented me a blue T-shirt with the words I CAN DO emblazoned across the front in large, bold letters. Those words translate what living in the present is all about. They stand in direct contrast to the first two attitudes, "If only I had . . ." and "What if . . .?" The words I CAN DO challenge you to accept responsibility for your life and start your renewal *now*.

The "I Can Do's" usually begin with small things: small plans, small challenges, small triumphs. As these small successes build in your life, you begin to feel good about yourself and the progress you have made.

Greg, a man in one of my recent workshops summed it up. "The road back is full of potholes and mountains," he said. "It is definitely more fun climbing mountains than falling into potholes."

We find Paul's "I can do" statement in Philippians 4:13, "I can do all things in Him who strengthens me." Paul was a rebuilder. He was a "right now" live-er infused with God's strength.

What are your "I can do's"? Have you taken time lately to write them down? Are you saying, "I can go back to school"; "I can find a new career"; "I can do a good job of single parenting"; "I can be responsible for myself"; "I can rebuild and go on with my life"?

Sometimes it is tempting to hunt for that special someone who already has a game plan going in his or her own life. But no one else can do your rebuilding for you. If you were a dependent person in your past marriage, you'll tend to search for a someone who will do everything for you. Many second marriages start on this premise, and many of them fail. Healthy marriages consist of an interdependent relationship.

Transition Means Change

How comfortable are you with change? Most of us feel pretty nervous and uncertain about it. The road into the world of single-again adults is littered with uncertainties. It can be intimidating, considering all the negative things you might have read or heard about the singles scene. However, you can't return to yesterday. You must move ahead, even though you would like to run and hide.

The Bible gives us an account in John 5 that demonstrates how radical change can be. Jesus singled out a man by the pool of Bethesda who had been ill for 38 years. He asked the man a strange yet probing question, "Do you want to get well again?" (Jn. 5:6, Phillips)

If someone had asked you that question the last time you had the flu, you know what you would have answered. Yet this man didn't seem to understand the question. Instead of a loud yes, the invalid told Jesus that he didn't understand his problem. In response, Jesus instantly healed the man and sent him on his way to a new life. Perhaps what Jesus was really asking was, "Do you want to make sweeping changes in your life?" To go from chronic sickness to total health would be a big change in anyone's life. Jesus seemed to be saying there would be a cost involved in the change. As I think about this incident, several aspects of the cost of change come to mind.

First, the man by the pool had to give up what was familiar. To all who used the pool, the man seemed to be a permanent fixture. His identity was connected to his illness. He seemed to belong there; he was a common sight. However, in order to get well, to change, he had to leave this familiar setting. That must have been frightening.

Second, the invalid had to give up the security he had found in his pool-side residency and sickness. He knew the people by the pool, and he knew the healing powers of the water. That gave him a sense of security.

Sometimes even sickness can be a security blanket that keeps us from changing. We can pull our bad situation or unfair circumstance around us and use it to shield against any new adventure or growth. Security can come in many forms. Are you afraid to let go of the familiar so that you can make some gains?

Third, the man had to move into a situation he knew little about. Lack of knowledge can be a justifiable fear. That fear is removed, however, when we do our homework and start exploring. The man by the pool had been sick so long that being well was strange territory.

For many single-again people, being on their own feels uncomfortable and unfamiliar. It may seem as if a cruel trick has been played on them. A time machine has thrust them backward to their late teens or early twenties; the only difference is that they no longer look 21.

In the Old Testament, God called Moses out of his semi-retirement lifestyle of minding his father-in-law Jethro's flocks. In the burning-bush conversation, Moses expressed his fear to God about leading the Israelites out of their bondage. God's promise to Moses was that He would go with him into Egypt and give him the words to speak and the ability to be a leader. Moses was still fearful. But he went, and God fulfilled His promise.

For the formerly married, singleness is a mystifying land. When they left singleness for marriage, they never expected to return there. Moses never planned to go back to Egypt. He left for good (or so he thought). For Moses, going back could have been accomplished only with the help of God. Asking for God's help in this single-again land can give you a new sense of direction and confidence.

Fourth, the man by the pool risked discovering who he really was. For 38 years, he lived with one identity, his illness. Now all that changed. Who would he be in his new role? Would he be accepted, loved, and understood? What would people think of him?

Self-discovery usually comes from the inside out. As outward conditions change, we reach inside ourselves to discover who we really are. One thing is certain: all of us are changing—caught in the process of becoming.

Many single-again people wonder who they are. Some have told me they have no identity in singleness and can't wait to remarry. But identity doesn't come in duets. As a single-again person, you are changing and getting in touch with yourself. Things are no longer as they once were. You are discovering yourself apart from marriage.

Fifth, the man by the pool faced rejection. I'm sure his new and healthy state drew many reactions from those around him. Perhaps his companions by the pool were so envious of his new life that they no longer wanted his friendship. Skepticism about how he was healed could also have turned some healthy people away from him. Instead of celebrating his healing, they questioned it. Instead of affirming him, they withdrew. The invalid could have easily been a man caught between two worlds and rejected by both.

Many single-again people can identify with this feeling. When you're going through change, you make those around you nervous. Sometimes people find it easier to avoid you than to affirm you. Longtime friends you had when you were married disappear. Even relatives can become a part of the vanishing community you once knew. It may make you want to escape the rejection by entering into a new, instant relationship that leads to the marriage altar.

Divorced people often feel a strong sense of rejection. If your mate left you for another person, rejection, self-doubt, and lack of self-esteem may threaten to stifle any attempts you make to rebuild your life.

Even the typical singles community may send out waves of rejection to the person trying to enter it. Once you do enter, you may experience individual rejection during the dating-mating-relating process. It's little wonder that many singles choose to hide out rather than reach out.

Few of us, single or married, ever learn how to handle rejection with any amount of finesse. We bruise easily and bleed freely, heal slowly and move ahead warily.

The last area the man by the pool had to deal with was a change in lifestyle. With a few words spoken by Jesus, his old life was gone. He could not stay in residence by the pool after he was well. He was thrust into a new lifestyle.

Much has been written about the single lifestyle. Depending on where you do your reading, it may be summed up as "swinging singles," "headhunters in a land of search and seizure," "the invasion of the body snatchers," "losers and misfits," and "loners and lepers."

The truth is, single-again people are just normal people. Changing one's marital status does not turn one into a two-headed monster. The thousands of singles I meet across America are simply looking for a pathway through singleness. They're trying to accept it as a part of life rather than a rough spot between marriages or a place to simply stagnate until rescued.

One of the most profound yet simple scriptural encouragements for living through the single state is found in Paul's letter to the Philippians. From his prison cell Paul said, "I have learned to be content, whatever the circumstances may be" (Phil. 4:11, Phillips). Paul had many things going for him. His life was exciting. But at the height of everything, he was thrown in jail. He had it all and lost it all. However, Paul's secret of contentment was to trust Christ in every situation. Christ's presence filled every nook and cranny of Paul's life. He never suffered from "situation vacillation." He learned to trust God and rest in the process.

Where Are You?

By now you may be comparing your life changes to those of the man by the pool of Bethesda. He was introduced to a new life. You were too. He didn't have a choice. Perhaps neither did you. His fears and challenges were equally divided. So are yours.

Where are you as you face the changes sudden singleness has brought your way? You may have moved beyond your crisis, but are you moving down the road of growth? I want to offer four questions to help you further evaluate your status and get a grip on personal growth. Don't simply read the questions. Spend some time with them. They demand some homework. Think carefully about each one.

1. Where am I now? If you don't know where you are, you won't know where you're going. Evaluate the mental, physical, emotional, spiritual, vocational, practical, and social areas of your life.

Are you making progress in the above areas? Are you stalled in some, while moving ahead in others? What are your priorities for growth in each area? After you make a list of where you feel you are in each one, make a second list of where you want to be and what it will take to get there. Before you start asking others for their opinions, write down your own opinions first. Start with acknowledging your feelings, and be honest.

2. Who am I now? The tendency is to answer this question by describing who you *were* rather than who you *are* right now. In the Scriptures, God sometimes gave His servants new names that described the kind of person they had become. Their challenge was to live up to the new name and build a new identity.

"Who am I now?" is a question of feeling and exploration. It encourages building and expanding a little each day. Sometimes that growth is best expressed by being able to say out loud, "I am single." It's much easier to say "I'm widowed" or "I'm divorced" than to say "I'm single."

Hanging like a rainbow over all you *think* you are is what God *knows* you are—loved by Him.

3. Where do I go from here? I always ask for directions when I travel—I want to know the quickest and easiest route to my destination. Sometimes, however, people neglect to mention detours. Detours take time, are seldom enjoyable, and are definitely inconvenient. But sometimes they're part of the journey.

Sudden singleness can seem like an eternal detour, but only if you choose to park by the sign. Getting the directions requires making plans and having goals. Others can point you in the right direction, but you have to take the journey.

4. How do I get there? A street-wise young man in New York was once asked the directions to Carnegie Hall. His response was, "Practice, man, practice." No one can do your practicing for you. Many single-again people have no destination and no means of getting anywhere.

In my 20 years of working with single people, I've spent some of the happiest times listening to stories of goals realized and achievements accomplished. In my divorce-recovery workshops, I often meet people at the crisis point in their lives. Their most important concern? To continue breathing. What a serendipity to meet them a year or two later and share in their progress and victories! I hear them say:

"I went back to school."
"I got that job."
"I moved and bought my own house."
"I joined a good singles group."
"I'm making it on my own."

Are you in transition or completely out of commission? At certain times, you'll feel as if not much is coming together for you. That's normal, because changes don't always follow predictable patterns. Most of us desire to "have it all together." We somehow think that this would prove to the rest of the world we are okay. Some of us readily identify with the saying, "I've got it all together, but I forgot where I put it."

Getting it together is a lifelong process. Making changes is a part of that process. Don't hide behind your fears. Look at your options and opportunities as you make decisions.

Life is like driving on the freeway. You're always changing lanes and rediscovering who you are in a situation where fear and adventure are new traveling companions.

Assessing Personal Growth

(Meet with a small group or at least one other person as you work through this section.)

1. Write down your three biggest "If only I hads."
2. Explain your three biggest "What ifs."
3. Name three things you can do to grow personally.
4. What are two of the biggest changes in your life over the past year?
5. With which of the six changes in the life of the man Jesus healed do you most identify? Why?

Chapter
Two

I Don't Know Who I Am

"Left to yourself, you're a problem.
But left to God, you're a possibility."

E. Stanley Jones

Moving from the world of the married to the world of the suddenly single again can cause an identity crisis. Marriage offers a cocoon of security. It means belonging to someone special and to the community of the married. It means being surrounded by people who affirm that you belong there. Suddenly that world collapses, and you're thrown into a world that seems to belong to another galaxy.

A basic fear that many single-again people face is having to start all over again after they have accumulated 20 or 30 years of marital experience. In this sense, starting over can mean many things. The most fearful seems to be relating to members of the opposite sex through dating. As Janet described it, "The only difference between being single at 45 and single at 18 is that at 45, you aren't fighting pimples any longer." The thought of having a second adolescence isn't very comforting. Most people feel that going through it once is enough!

Building a new identity as a single-again person raises many questions and provides few responses. I want to ask some of those questions and try to offer helpful answers.

9

Why Am I Afraid of the Word *Single?*

The word *single* is fine for a person under 25 years old. Above that age, singleness can be perceived as failure to the bearer and to others in his or her life. Society still seems to feel that people come in pairs. And those who are paired feel most at ease around others who are paired. If you are never married, and over 25, you may face speculation as to why you're still single. The "how come" seems to spring up frequently.

If the word *single* is a problem to the never married, it is even more of a problem to the formerly married. The "how come" is replaced by the "I wonder what happened." You may spend hours planning an answer so you can respond when asked. You may want to say that yes, you're single, but unlike all those other single-again people out there. You and your situation are different from the other 70 million single people. As a single-again person, you "want an identity, but don't want to identify with others."

I meet many singles who steadfastly refuse to attend any singles groups or singles functions. I know of a church that has over 800 singles on the rolls; yet less than a third of that number are involved in the singles ministry. Sometimes, it's because of a bad first experience in a singles group.

Perhaps you have conjured up your own somewhat distorted ideas of who other singles are and how they feel. Have you given them a chance? Better yet, have you given yourself a chance with them? Desperately clinging to a married mentality will not help you accept your new single state.

Singleness is simply a part of your journey through life, much like childhood and adolescence were. Singleness isn't a disease that can be cured by death or marriage; neither is it a holding pattern.

Many singles have shared with me their feelings about singleness. The ones who are really growing and dealing with their single identity are the ones who can say, "It's not where I meant to be in my life, and it's not where I want to be, but I accept it and will use it as a place to grow."

Don't be afraid of the word *single*. It isn't synonymous with failure. Don't let others put you into an identity box because of what their image of singleness is. Singleness isn't a place to hide until someone discovers you and spirits you away to the marriage altar. It's your place to live and grow.

Do I Have to Spend All My Singleness with Single People?

I certainly hope not. I hear many complaints that single people feel isolated from other groups, particularly in church life. Singles groups, fellowships, and socials do not attempt to herd all the single people together in an isolation ward. They honestly work to meet the needs of single people and provide a place of fellowship and growth for them. You need friendships with fellow strugglers. There will always be special times for inclusion with other groups and for exclusion with your own group. Both are important in the single person's life.

It's human nature to move with the people who are interested in the things we find important. Many times close friendships develop from shared interests. Single-again people who are ready to build new and meaningful relationships want to spend time with other singles. Find your own balance in this area and begin to reach out to others.

What If I Never Remarry?

Katherine, an attractive and poised woman in her late 50s approached me at the end of a singles conference. She led me to a quiet corner of the room and asked a question I've heard hundreds of times before, "Where are all the good men my age?"

Sometimes I jokingly reply, "Anchorage, Alaska, the last frontier."

It's a question that has no easy answers. A single-again person under the age of 35 doesn't seem to worry as much about finding someone to remarry as a person over 40 does. For many reasons, the field of likely candidates narrows dramatically as age increases.

First, many men in their 50s want to date and relate to women in their 30s or 40s. Whether or not you think this is an ego problem is unimportant. The fact is, it's a social reality. Thinking that it's unfair doesn't help the problem. It simply exists.

Second, men over 50 tend to die off more rapidly than women that age.

Third, men find it more difficult to join social groups than women do. Women tend to be more relational, while men tend to be more vocational and occupational.

Fourth, men are expected to initiate relationships with women, while women are expected to wait for their invitation. There are exceptions to this social rule, expecially among younger people, but the old standard still holds for most. When a man has a lot of choices, a woman may find herself spending time on the bench, waiting to be invited into the game.

The reality is that many men and women who have lost a mate by death or divorce will never remarry. That may sound like a very negative and lonely statement, but facing and dealing with reality produces more growth than living in a fantasy. Building relationships on all levels is important for the single person. Those relationships aren't intended to take the place of your former spouse; they simply add meaning, purpose, and a caring community to your life. We all need a place to belong.

Is It Normal to Really Like Being Single Again?

I meet many singles during the crisis point in their loss of a mate. They tell me they'll never survive the loss. Many expect to die. When I see them a few years later, they've made the difficult adjustment and are growing. Eventually, some really enjoy the freedom that singleness has brought into their lives. They can come and go as they please, have many new friends, and feel a sense of contentment. This doesn't necessarily mean they're committed to singleness forever. Some have said they would remarry if the right person came along. But they've left behind the quest for marriage and the frantic searching that is sometimes a part of the singles world. This is especially true of many singles whose children are grown and gone from home. Many older singles have found the delicate balance between freedom and loneliness, finding peace in their single-again status.

What Do I Do If I Really Want to Remarry?

Debbie told me she recently placed an ad in a singles newspaper. She thought if she described herself and the type of man she wanted to meet, she'd find the right person. After numerous responses and dates, Debbie declared the whole venture a disaster. Her reason for doing it was desperation—she wasn't meeting any available men in her world.

Newspapers and magazines are filled with countless ways to meet available singles. Many single-again people wonder whether or not they should enter the match-a-mate game. Many of those who have find it a stilted way to meet people and are dissatisfied with the results.

If you're wondering about whether or not to use this method, ask for God's guidance as you consider if you really want to remarry—assuming that you're emotionally ready and have biblical permission to do so. If you're ready, you need to affirm it to yourself. Self-affirmation is the first positive step.

After you've made that decision, you must be able to share it with your close and trusted friends. Some single-again people try to play the game of "Pretend you don't want to get married and someone will try to convince you that you should." You waste a lot of good energy playing games. Being honest about your feelings will help you, and let others know where you're coming from.

It's normal to want to remarry and to know that you're ready for it.

There's also nothing wrong with sharing that with others. Just don't print it on your new T-shirt!

Don't be concerned about scaring off prospects with your honesty. If you can frighten them away, let them run. Anyone who needs convincing is an unlikely candidate anyhow.

Often, women ask me what I think about a woman asking a man over for dinner. I think it's a great idea! Women should have the freedom to take this kind of initiative once in a while. I know some men who are waiting to be asked out. They are just as afraid of asking as women are. Believe it or not, men fear rejection too.

While it's fine to reveal your intentions, don't come on too strong. Let relationships grow naturally. If they're meant to blossom, they will. If they appear to be dying, don't throw more fertilizer on them. Move on and don't be discouraged. Talking someone into a relationship can be hazardous to your health. Remember, you need to approach remarriage carefully; as high as 68 percent of them fail.

If you want to remarry, the wisest thing to do is to let God know about it, and ask for His guidance and help in finding the right person. I don't believe you should spend all your time sitting at home, rocking and praying about it; but I do think you should rock, pray, and then raise your antenna. If it's God's will, someone will be out there!

Taking a Close-up Look at a New Identity

Joining a new group, playing for a new team, moving to a new town, and starting a new job all can be a part of entering the world of sudden singleness. How well you succeed in this arena depends largely on how you feel about yourself. Your self-esteem is an axis upon which your new life will balance. Here are three questions that give will you a closer look at your new identity.

1. How do you see yourself? Every morning you look into the mirror. What do you see? Are you discouraged by your appearance—thinning hair, sagging stomach, multiplying wrinkles? Perhaps everything seems to be in a conspiracy to destroy your self-image. Oh, to be 25 years old again and a Mr. or Miss America!

You can take one of two approaches to what you see in the mirror. You can say, "All right," or you can say, "All wrong." (A third alternative would be to break the mirror!)

If you don't accept what you see in the mirror, you will project those feelings of self-doubt all day long. Your thoughts will be consumed by what you wish you looked like. You might even spend hundreds of dollars and hours of time in a personal rehabilitation project to improve your self-image.

On the other hand, if you're comfortable with what you see in the mirror, you'll convey that to those around you.

So how do you help yourself? Do you just keep on wishing? No, you begin by accepting yourself. This doesn't mean you're stuck. You can make physical changes if you desire. But your basic attitude will say, "Thank You, God, for the gift of me. I accept the gift and thank You for it."

I meet singles in my travels who wish they were married. I meet some marrieds who wish they were single. I meet poor people who wish they were rich and rich people who wish they were richer. You can spend a great deal of time wishing you were different; wanting to change the physical is just one side of self-image.

I sometimes ask the people I counsel how they feel about themselves. Immediately, they point out specific reasons why they don't feel good about who they are. Physical appearance is often a leading cause (too fat, too thin). Lack of material possessions (money) is a close second, followed by personal problems (shyness, no friends). Too often, people concentrate on what's wrong rather than on what they can change and improve. Some days it seems that 90 percent of the singles I meet suffer from a poor self-image.

To counteract this, singles must practice believing the truth. You are God's unique, unrepeatable miracle. God does not deal in junk! You are very special, no matter how you think you look in the mirror.

2. How do others see you? That's a tricky one. Even if you have a fairly positive self-image, you always wonder if others like what they see. In order to enhance this perception, many people spend all their time trying to please others. Some even attempt to buy approval.

I went to school with a very obnoxious boy named Billy who didn't appeal to his classmates. Knowing this, he tried to buy their acceptance by inviting them every day after school to be his guests at the local snack shop. Billy worked desperately to purchase friendship. The sad thing was that his schoolmates enjoyed his treats but rejected his friendship when he wasn't buying. It was a tragic experience for Billy, but it happens all the time. You simply can't buy approval.

One way to help others see us better is to concentrate on being ourselves. The old television show "Candid Camera," used the slogan, "People caught in the act of being themselves." There is freedom in being ourselves. Maybe the biggest discovery any of us can make is to know who we really are and to be true to that person.

I once worked as singles pastor at a church in Hollywood, California. To many, Hollywood is known as the land of plastic impressions and relationships. Many who live there are so caught up in the act of selling their image to others that they've forgotten what lies beneath. As a result, what others see in them may not be what they get.

Sometimes people judge us by how honest we are. A good relationship with another person always starts by telling the truth about ourselves. When we carry that into every area of our lives, others will see us as trustworthy. We need to be honest with God, with others, and with ourselves.

People also view us in the way we do or don't affirm others. A lot has been written about the importance of affirming children. For example, if a child comes home from school with a mammoth hunk of butcher paper covered with finger painting, the parent says kind and affirming things about both the art work and the artist, and puts the picture on the refrigerator door. The parent doesn't throw it in the trash and inform the child the drawing is terrible.

In the same way, adults need to hear someone say out loud, "You did well," or as they say down South, "You done good!" Encouragement to do greater things comes from the affirmation we receive in doing the smaller ones. We all need recognition. Do others see you as an affirmer?

3. How does God see you? Many divorced people would say that God sees them only as sinners, since divorce is a sin. They feel a hopelessness that affects other areas of their lives and may produce a negative self-image. They forget that God is in the forgiveness business.

John 3:16 tells us that God loved the world. We are in that world and a vital part of it. God sees us as His creation and His children—we're a part of His family. He also views us as forgiven creatures. We are recipients of God's unconditional, unlimited love.

Sometimes you run into people who want to tell you how they think God sees you. When you meet them, take a quick walk in the opposite direction. When you know how God sees you and can verify it from the Scriptures, you won't need their interpretations or judgments. As your new identity slowly comes into focus, you should be able to shout, "I am single, I am special, I am loved by God!"

Getting My New Identity in Gear

There's a portion of Scripture in Philippians 4 that must have been written with a few singles in mind. In this passage, Paul sets forth three concepts that helped him in his own growth and self-identity.

The first principle is learning to accept your circumstances. In Philippians 4:11 Paul says, "Not that I complain of want; for I have learned, in whatever state I am, to be content."

Paul made this statement despite what he'd gone through: numerous shipwrecks, angry mobs, trials and imprisonments, questions about his leadership by his own people. Paul knew what he was talking about. He was seldom away from crisis. Somehow, though, God gave Paul a spirit of confidence to know that where he was at any given moment was right—not always comfortable, but right.

To deal more effectively with your singleness, you have to accept it for now. Peace comes with acceptance and the knowledge that God is with you in your situation. You are not alone! Many days you'll look toward heaven and want to shout, "Why me, Lord?" If you listen, you might hear an answer, "Why not you? I will give you the strength you need."

The second principle Paul offers is to grow where God's placed you. We've all heard the little instruction, "Bloom where you're planted." Sometimes we'd rather take our garden and move to an easier place to flower.

Paul showed strength by doing some of his blooming while in prison. He longed to be free, but he used the experience to win some of his captors to faith in Christ. His secret is in verse 13, "I can do all things in Him who strengthens me." Paul didn't grow on his own; God infused him daily with the strength he needed. That same growth-producing strength is available to you.

Some single-again people think they'll put off growing until they feel better or their circumstances change. But all that does is encourage stagnation. Other singles wait to be rescued. Their hope is that they won't have to work too hard if someone else will do their growing for them. The real truth is, however, that you have to do your own growing. No one else can do it for you.

The third principle Paul talks about is building. In verse 19 he says, "And my God will supply every need of yours according to His riches in glory in Christ Jesus." You can't build anything until God supplies you with the materials. They may not be the tools you want, but God will give you all the things that you need.

Many single-again people tell me they can't move ahead with their lives because they don't have everything they had before singleness interrupted their journey. The problem is that they see what they *don't* have rather than what God *does* have.

Matthew 6:31 tells us, "Therefore do not be anxious, saying, 'What shall we eat?' or 'What shall we drink?' or 'What will we wear?'" The writer goes on to say, "But seek first His kingdom and all these things shall be yours as well" (v. 33).

Accepting who you are, growing where you are, and building with what God has supplied you, are crucial to creating a new identity as a single-now person. We don't abandon what formed our identities in the first place—our family of origin, education, vocation, friends, lifestyle, faith, values. The old and the new come together to increase our self-discovery.

No matter what's in the past or on the horizon, we can claim with assurance the verse in Jeremiah 29:11, "'I know the plans I have for you' says the Lord. 'They are plans for good and not for evil, plans to give you a future and a hope.'"

Assessing Personal Growth

1. When you tell people you're single, how do they usually respond?
2. How do you feel if their response is negative?
3. What is the most difficult thing you face in being single again?
4. Name one or two things you like most about being single.
5. Describe one or two things you're doing to get your singleness in gear.

I'm So Lonely
I Could Die

*"Loneliness is not a disease cured by a never-ending
string of new relationships."*

Last year, 286,987 people died of loneliness. A shocking statistic. "I never heard that before," you say. You probably didn't for two reasons. First, no one keeps that kind of count. Second, few people, if any, die of loneliness—at least in a physical sense. I suspect, however, that hundreds of thousands of people die a little emotionally each year as a result of loneliness.

In a recent seminar with over 250 singles, I asked the participants to write a one-word description of their greatest fear. As I tallied the cards while flying home after the seminar, I was shocked to find the vast majority had written the word *loneliness*.

Although loneliness is an experience everyone goes through at one time or another, the acute sting of it is somehow more real to those who've become suddenly single again.

During a recent counseling session, Chris confessed that he hated bars and drinking; yet, he spent most of his weekends at happy hour so he wouldn't have to face his empty apartment and the loss of his wife.

Some singles have even told me they spend a great deal of time wandering through shopping malls just looking for people to talk with.

19

Psychologists tell us there are three things that relieve loneliness and bring happiness to most people. They are: *something to do, someone to love, and something to look forward to.* Many of you reading this would probably say that the loss of your spouse has robbed you forever of these possibilities.

The reality of sudden singleness is that you'll feel lonely. It's normal. It's also true that you'll attempt to relieve that loneliness in a lot of crazy ways. Beth filled her apartment with singing birds. She had lots of noise and lots of cleaning up, but she soon found that you can't instantly replace a spouse with six canaries.

You can't replace your spouse with things or with another person. Loneliness must be experienced for what it is. You have to feel that loss and grief as a part of the growth process. You can't escape loneliness by over-socializing or going into seclusion and feeling sorry for yourself.

Sometimes we seek to fill the lonely silence with sound. It's not unlike the teenager who roars home from school, flies to his bedroom, and turns on the boom box full blast. After about 30 seconds of airwave shock, his parent asks him to turn it down or off. Most teenagers will say they don't like being in their room alone when it's quiet. The sound of rock music is, to them, the sound of people filling up the empty room.

We do the same thing. The first on-switch in our car after the ignition is the radio. We seldom drive anywhere in quiet lest we be reminded of the absence of people. Often, sounds are small life preservers that help us cope with loneliness.

There are many lonely people depicted in the Scriptures. Some of the leaders in the Old Testament found themselves lonely in their serving capacity. Some who tried to run from God's direction became the victims of loneliness. After one of his greatest victories for God, Elijah the prophet lay down under a bush, plagued by the desire to die. He was lonely and fearful, and it wasn't until God came to him that his loneliness began to pass.

Moses experienced isolation and loneliness while leading the Israelites around in the wilderness. Jesus experienced the loneliness of going to the cross alone. The lines from a Negro spiritual express much of His life. The song laments, "Jesus walked this lonesome valley, He had to walk it by Himself. Oh, nobody else could walk it for Him, He had to walk it by Himself."

Some of your journey through singles territory will be very lonely. I don't know if there's a lonelier experience than your first time at a singles meeting. Just by placing your body in the room, you're saying, "I'm single." Fear of rejection by those already there can be pretty strong. It's easy to feel that you're just one more lonely person in a room full of lonely people.

As difficult as it is to feel alone, let me offer you a reality check about loneliness:

1. I will experience loneliness as a newly single person.
2. It's normal to feel lonely.
3. I won't die of loneliness.
4. Substitutions won't dissolve my loneliness.
5. I'll grow through encountering loneliness.

My experience as a counselor has revealed two distinct kinds of loneliness for the newly single person. *The first relates to the person no longer in your life, due to death or divorce.* Feelings range from wishing it were *not* so to anger that it *is* so. You may go from fantasizing to attempting to fill your memory. Healing finally begins when time passes, and you are honest in facing and working through your feelings.

*The second kind of loneliness deals with wanting another person, almost any other person, in your life—*someone who will be there for you and bring meaning to your existence, someone to whom you will be significant.

One of the greatest struggles in sudden singleness is dealing with this kind of loneliness. Some respond to it by engaging in an endless chain of sexual relationships. Others go from singles meeting to singles meeting looking for someone to fill their void of loneliness. These types of relationships never satisfy for long.

Negative Responses to Loneliness

There are as many responses to loneliness as there are people who are lonely. Here are some negative reactions.

1. Run away and hide. If you do this, you won't have to face the problem. Or even better, people will feel sorry for you and do the things for you that you need to do for yourself.

Emotional running is an increasing problem in our society. Our very mobility encourages it. But can you ever run far enough to get away from loneliness?

2. Pop a pill. Got a headache? Take an aspirin. Got a heartache? Take a valium. Drug dependency is a common way of resolving almost any mental, psychological, emotional, or physical problem. As we run from reality, the pile of pills grows higher. Uppers, downers, lifters, levelers. Are you hooked on pills as a way to handle your loneliness?

3. Eat six hot-fudge sundaes and a giant pizza. Probably all of us, at one time or another, have raided the refrigerator in a moment of depression, anxiety, or loneliness. Did we feel better afterward? Generally not. The truth is, you can't eat your problems away, even if your salivary glands seem to be saying that you can. Are you trying to eat your way through loneliness? What will you look like if you do? What will your self-image be?

4. Feel sorry for yourself. Once you have taken up residence in Pity City, your next move can be into the Valley of Depression. There are hundreds of books in print that deal with depression and how to cure it. Perhaps the best way to prevent depression is to watch for the road signs leading to it and turn the other way.

Self-pity usually starts by you telling yourself that what happened to you is unfair. The implication is that it should've happened to someone else; you certainly didn't deserve it. After you tell yourself that long enough, you start telling it to others. All they have to do is confirm it, tell you they agree with you, and you are on the freeway to Pity City. Depression, the ultimate destination of many singles, becomes a cocoon in which to hide from life. It's the final prison of self-commiseration. How much time each week do you spend feeling sorry for yourself?

5. Become a social butterfly. I meet many singles who try to replace their loneliness with an enormous amount of activity. There's nothing wrong with staying busy if you aren't hiding behind it. It's only when activities keep you from facing your own struggles that they take on a negative dimension. I asked one suddenly single-again cyclone, Joan, if she ever slowed down or stopped long enough to catch her breath. Joan's response? "If I do, I'm afraid of what I'll find out." Coming, going, and doing in turbo-fashion will more quickly result in fatigue than in a cure for loneliness.

6. Go on a buying spree. Women are often accused of buying new clothing to make themselves feel better. All of us have had the experience of purchasing something we didn't need or really want in order to ease the hurt or frustration of a situation. To be sure, it's a momentary high. The problem is that it doesn't last, and the original problem still remains. Will a bigger house, a sportier car, a new wardrobe, a younger man or woman, a month in Europe really solve your loneliness problem? Are they answers or just minimal temporary relief?

Some Positive Responses to Loneliness

This isn't a "do it and you will be fine" list. Some singles have found the following suggestions helpful, but they've had to work at them to find success.

1. Find a place to belong. Most healthy relationships are built within the walls of a supportive community. Moving from the married world via a spouse's death or divorce usually sends you in search of a new support structure. Many people feel they no longer belong to the world of the married or the single.

There's a place for you to belong as a single-again person. There are singles groups, singles clubs, singles tours, singles seminars and conferences, singles apartment complexes. There's no shortage of places and things that cater to singles. Some may be good for you, others may not. Reality is that you do need a special place to belong. It may take some searching and some time. But you'll know you've found your place when some of your loneliness subsides.

2. Give your self-esteem a shot in the arm. Many of the single people I meet around the country have low self-esteem. Some have experienced rejection to the point that they believe they're worthless. Don't fall into this mode of thinking! No matter what you've gone through, you are still God's unique, unrepeatable miracle.

In the Scriptures, Peter's self-esteem was at a very low point after he denied Christ. It took an upper-room encounter and a preaching experience later on to renew Peter's belief in himself as well as his belief in God.

A friend of mine has a favorite saying. When I leave him he always admonishes, "Stay well and be good to yourself." Most of us don't have any problem with the staying well part. A daily dose of vitamins and a good exercise routine will take care of that. The second part is a little more difficult, though. Being good to ourselves means recognizing that we are worth something, that we deserve happiness.

The Bible speaks about loving your neighbor as yourself. You must love yourself. At its finest point, that's what self-esteem is all about. Succeeding at a new challenge and making changes in your life all contribute to your self-esteem. What have you done for yourself lately that has made you feel good?

3. Get into the physical. Krista, clad in a jogging suit and running shoes, dropped into a front-row chair in my seminar. I asked her if she ran. Krista's breathless response was, "Ran all the way over here this morning. Several miles. Plan to run home when we're finished. Never ran until my divorce. Needed to get out of the pits. Been running ever since."

Obviously, running isn't the answer for everyone, but it does have its advantages. Participating in physical activities gets the body moving. Exercise demands something from you even when you don't feel like giving it. Your mind and your body are interconnected. It's difficult to feel lonely and sorry for yourself after you've just run two or three miles. You can also enjoy sports with others. Take some lessons if needed. Just get yourself moving!

4. Set some goals. The motto on a wall plaque says, "Shoot at nothing and that's exactly what you will hit." Many newly single people lack goals. If they do have some, the goals are contingent, based upon someone else's reaction, response, or plans. Working toward a goal gives purpose and meaning to our everyday lives. Writing this book didn't happen until I set the goal and then began to implement it a day at a time.

I've always dreamed of running in a marathon, but I only dream about the start and finish. It's hard to dream about the agony of what lies between. I know that in order for me to reach that goal, I need to set apart time to train. Training means running from 50 to 60 miles a week. That's the catch. I don't want to take the time to run that far each week. So I run a couple of miles a day and keep on dreaming.

If you're going to set some goals, set attainable ones first. Aim for the big ones later. When you reach one of your goals, always celebrate. You deserve the party!

5. Get some help. If your loneliness seems to be a prison and you feel unable to escape, don't hesitate to get some professional counseling. Sometimes the roots of loneliness are tied to other things in our lives, and only therapy can bring some resolution to the struggle. Don't be afraid to look for answers in the skills of others. And remember, counseling takes time. There are no instant answers to problems that may have accrued over a period of years.

6. Talk to God about it. God is aware of all the difficulties a person can have. Back in the Garden of Eden, God recognized one of Adam's original needs. He said, "It is not good that the man should be alone; I will make him a help mate for him" (Gen. 2:18, KJV). Some of you will read this and say, "I wish it were that easy. Just ask God and—zap! The loneliness is gone!"

God is aware of our loneliness. It is and always has been a part of the human condition. But God can move in different ways in our lives when we invite Him to fill some of the lonely void.

His first promise to us was set in cement. The writer of Hebrews put it this way, "I will in no wise fail thee, Neither will I in any wise forsake thee" (Heb. 13:5, Phillips). In your loneliness and mine, God is right there, backing us up with His promises. He isn't moving out on us, divorcing us, or dying on us. He is there! He doesn't always do things on our timetable. Our schedule usually dictates, RIGHT NOW. God seems to say, *When I am ready, then you will be ready.*

Sharing your needs, your struggles, and your loneliness with God in prayer is a positive step. Inviting God to help meet those needs in His own way is another step. Here is a short prayer you can say:

God, I'm so lonely. I know that's human. I invite You to come with Your strength, power, and love into the very center of my loneliness. Sweep away the cobwebs that tie me up, and help me to start climbing the ladder of growth. Amen.

Loneliness is the feeling that you're alone on the journey through life and no one cares about your joys and sorrows. Perhaps someone once did, but he or she is no longer around.

Working through your loneliness is a time of rebuilding, when you can evaluate and sort things out, by looking deep inside yourself. It's a special time for reflection, meditation, and future planning. Dealing with loneliness means turning a negative experience into a positive, growth-producing one. It means developing a plan that won't leave you stuck at the crossroads of loneliness and self-pity.

Loneliness can be a rare gift that keeps us in touch with our humanity. It moves us toward a deeper relationship with God and our neighbors. Loneliness will always be a part of the experience for the suddenly single-again person. Instead of a liability, however, it can be a great gift from God that enables you to grow.

Assessing Personal Growth

1. What's the loneliest thing about being single again?
2. At what time during the week do you feel most lonely?
3. When loneliness seems to trap you and push you toward depression, what do you usually do to resolve it?
4. Of the negative responses to loneliness listed in this chapter, which response do you most identify with?
5. Of the positive responses to loneliness listed, which response helps you the most?

I Need All the Friends
I Can Get

*"Friendship is the inexpressible comfort of feeling safe with a person,
having neither to weigh thoughts nor measure words."*

George Eliot

I n the last chapter, I suggested positive ways to handle the struggle with
loneliness. One of those ways was to find a place to belong—a supportive
and sustaining community.

In a book titled *Loneliness: The Experience of Emotional and Social
Isolation,* Robert Weiss explores the many problems of loneliness. In the last
pages of the book, he offers a solution to this haunting problem. He says:

> I can offer no method for ending loneliness other than the forma-
> tion of new relationships that might repair the deficit responsible for
> the loneliness. And I think this solution ordinarily is not easy. If it were,
> there would be fewer lonely people.[1]

Daniel Yankelovich, a researcher, says that the hunger for deeper personal
relationships shows up in his research findings as a growing conviction that a
me-first, satisfy-all-my-desires attitude leads to relationships that are superficial,
transitory, and ultimately unsatisfying. He found that 70 percent of Americans
recognize that while they have many acquaintances, they have few close

friends, and they experience that as a serious void in their lives. He learned that two out of five, 41 percent, said they have fewer close friends than they had in the recent past.

In the "Peanuts" comic strip, Charlie Brown makes a statement every so often that he needs all the friends he can get. When you examine the endless stream of characters drifting through Charlie's life, you quickly understand what he means. Charlie needs friends who won't pull the football away when he's about to kick it, and friendly trees that won't ensnare his kite when he flies it.

You and I aren't unlike good old Charlie Brown. We too need friends—good ones we can trust, understanding and caring ones who'll be there in any and every situation.

In the world of the suddenly single-again person, that ready-made "best friend," one's spouse, is no longer there. Sometimes, even the friends you made through your spouse disappear. At first, reaching out to others can feel extremely uncomfortable. Recognize that singleness is a time for relational rebuilding, and that's a slow process.

The Different Levels of Relationships

Most of us are inhibited enough to want others to do all the reaching out. That's usually safe, for it puts us in charge of the response we choose to make. When we reach out to others first, we run the risk of being rejected, which gives them control.

Here are several types of relationships we all encounter.

1. *Random relationships.* A great number of come-and-go relationships drift through our lives: the clerk at the supermarket who bags our groceries and exchanges small talk, the service-station mechanic we see every three months for car maintenance, the mailman and the paperboy, friends at church, our children's friends' parents. You could add a whole lot more to the list.

These are the surface people in our lives. Our conversations usually consist of "Hi, how are you?" "Fine, how are you?" These people serve our own needs at an operational level. We don't really want to know how they are, and we don't have time to find out. Even worse, we don't actually care, because our involvement with them is minimal. They're merely our "maintenance people." We know their names and faces but not their lives and struggles. We choose no deeper involvement with them than we already have.

2. *Social relationships.* There are also people in our lives with whom we

socialize. We bowl, party, picnic, vacation, and camp with them. We invest ourselves recreationally with this group, but we rarely relate on a deep emotional level.

Many single-again people have had the experience of going to a social event attended by couples who were once a part of their world. It doesn't take long for them to feel out of place. The visible togetherness of others accentuates their aloneness.

3. Deep relationships. In my seminars, I sometimes ask the question, "How many of you have had a deep, intimate relationship with someone other than your spouse, a relationship of over 10 years' endurance?" Usually not many hands raise, but most people express an honest desire for this in their lives.

In the Bible, David and Jonathan had a deep friendship. That didn't come about overnight. It took time to grow into an enduring relationship.

Few of us have the time to invest in more than one or two deep relationships. Our busy schedules push us toward an "instant intimacy" with other people. Our cry is, "Bare your soul. Tell me your history, and let's have a deep relationship." Friendships that are lasting and enduring don't happen this way. Our world is in a hurry, but you can't rush the growth of a significant relationship. Perhaps the line from Paul Simon's "59th Street Bridge Song" needs to be heard again: "Slow down, you move too fast. Got to make the morning last."

Deep relationships involve listening, sharing, caring, and a great deal of personal commitment. A relationship with depth is always a time investment.

We could call the three levels of relationship-building "stepping stones." All relationships begin on a random or casual level. We decide whether or not we'll elevate them from there to the social level. Once at the social level, we decide if we'll move toward intimacy or depth with that person.

There is some chemistry in all relationships. Both people have to invest equal energy in the relationship. One person alone can't make it happen. Sometimes our most meaningful relationships begin in strange ways. You can't plan them any more than you can set aside a day to go shopping for a new spouse. Relationships begin when we're available to them. Essentially, that means they won't happen if you're hiding in your closet or stuck in your rocker peering out the window at life passing by.

I meet some people who try to spiritualize their lack of good relationships by stating that God will send friends to them when He is ready. I deeply believe in God's direction in our lives, but I also feel we have to take the initiative and push ourselves out into the mainstream of life. Fishing in the bathtub can be a frustrating experience.

Let me clarify that in talking about relationship-building, we aren't talking about finding a spouse. We're discussing finding friends of both sexes. It's possible for a relationship to bloom into a marriage. That, however, would be a serendipity.

Building relationships indicates bringing meaningful people into your life at many different levels. Many single-again people have only one objective in mind: find someone to marry, as soon as possible. The pressure and panic that results from this kind of pursuit is enormous.

An alternate response to the marriage-partner search is to see how many relationships you can sustain while "playing the field." Having a "one-night stand" is sometimes synonymous with this kind of behavior. People are used and discarded for self-gratification rather than relationship-building.

When two people marry, they already have a relationship with one another. In-laws and relatives on both sides of the family form an instant circle of accepted relationships. Divorce and death can strip away this close circle and leave a person standing alone. Looking into the world of singleness means restructuring and building new and meaningful relationships.

Jesus' Circles of Relationships

Jesus is our model for relationship-building. We will gain more from looking at how He constructed and maintained relationships than how He survived as a single.

Relationships were important to Jesus, and He gave quality time to them. The closest and most intimate relationship Jesus had on earth appears to have been with John, the beloved disciple. Beyond His immediate family, John was a relationship priority with Jesus. Scriptures portray the deep love and intimacy between Jesus and John as a special friendship.

On another level, Peter, James, and John seemed to form the inner circle that Jesus kept close to Himself. He confided in and asked for special support from them. They were near Jesus in His moments of both triumph and agony. Each of the men was as different from the others as night and day. Yet their friendship with Jesus ran deep.

On other relationship levels, we have the 12 disciples; after that, the 70, the 120, and the 500 followers of Christ. Beyond all of these were the crowds that pursued Jesus everywhere. They reached out to touch Him and He touched them back. They went their way and He went His.

As you explore the Gospels, you can quickly see where Jesus spent most of His time. He knew He couldn't give quality time to everyone. The disciples were His inner circle. They shared in His life.

At yet another place in Jesus' friendship circle stood Mary, Martha, and Lazarus. Scripture indicates it was to their home that Jesus went for refuge, renewal, and rest. All of us need a retreat center like that—away from the demands of life, distant from the reaching hands of others and their constant expectations. We need a place and a circle of friends in which to relax and let down our guard. This is a very important part of relationship-building. Where is your special place to rest and be renewed while the world races by?

The Value of Deep Relationships

If the comment by researcher Yankelovich at the beginning of this chapter is true, perhaps we should take a look at the value of the relationships we need and what they'll add to our lives.

1. Acceptance. We all have a basic human need to be accepted by others as we are—warts and all. So we reveal only little bits and pieces of ourselves as we get to know others. We're testing them to see if there's a point of nonacceptance where they'll cut us off from going deeper in the relationship. Sometimes this is done adeptly in the dating process. We spend hours prepping for a date so that someone will see us as we'd like them to. It's only when we feel more accepted by the other person that we lower our preparation time. After marriage we usually give less thought to how we look to the other person.

As children we're told to make a good impression on people. We'll be liked and accepted if we do. This attitude follows us throughout adulthood. One day my doorbell rang, and I raced through the house from backyard gardening to answer it. As the sweat and dirt ran down my face, I opened the door, only to stand nose to nose with Amy, one of the most immaculately dressed women I'd ever known. She was in my church's singles group and had stopped by to drop off some fliers. Standing there in my cutoffs, shirtless and dripping, I certainly didn't look like anything close to a senior staff minister at a large church. Amy's comment, "Jim?" didn't mask her surprise. I found myself racing through an apology for the way I looked, explaining that I was knee-deep in gardening. I was desperately concerned that she wouldn't continue to accept me as her pastor because I didn't appear pastorly.

From time to time, we all get caught not looking the way we would like to. Life seems to be one long prep course in acceptance.

2. Trust. A deep relationship with another person requires trust as a root ingredient. Without trust, relationships are superficial. I speak with many people in divorce counseling who've had their trust violated. Perhaps their husbands or wives ran off with another person. They wonder if they'll ever be able to trust anyone again.

Trust is earned as a relationship or friendship grows. When a friend says he or she will pick you up at eight, you place trust in his or her commitment. If trust is constantly violated by habitual lateness, the confidence level goes down. Building trust is believing promises as you see them lived out.

God placed an infinite amount of faith in you and me as His creative work. We return that trust by believing His Word and accepting the promises it contains. Our confidence in God grows as we watch those promises being fulfilled in our lives. When God says He's with us, He's really with us! A deep relationship with a friend affirms, "I literally trust you with my life." A deep relationship with God says the same thing.

3. Lack of jealousy. Can you have a deep and meaningful relationship with someone you're jealous of? I don't believe you can. Jealousy becomes a noose around a relationship, strangling the life from it. Envy ran rampant in the early Church. Paul constantly spoke about it in his letters. Even the disciples had to deal with jealousy as they struggled for the highest position in the kingdom they thought Jesus was setting up on earth.

Jealousy is a part of our human condition, but it destroys relationships. Celebration must replace envy. Instead of being jealous of my friends' gifts, talents, promotions, success, and wealth, I can choose to rejoice in them. If I want the best for my friends, I'll realize I am not in competition, but in friendship with them.

4. Honesty. When faced with a conflict or a decision, it's easy to go from friend to friend collecting opinions. This is usually a "pooling of ignorance." Most of the time we're just listening for what we want to hear. Few of us tell the truth to others. We're afraid that if we do, our relationships with them will falter and end.

Scripture says, "Speak the truth in love" (Eph. 4:15, Phillips). Truth, when spoken, demands a gentle touch. It's not something we throw at people and hope they will catch. It's fragile. Only our real friends, those who love us most, will tell us the truth. Honesty always hurts significantly less when it comes from someone who loves us and whom we love in return.

5. Loyalty. When we're loyal to someone, we send the message, "I will stand with you no matter what. If you do something I disagree with, I will tell you, but I will still be loyal to you with my friendship." Some of the best outward expressions of loyalty seem to come from animals. The world could certainly use a few more Lassies, Silvers, and Old Paints. Loyalty cements friendship.

The one thing Jesus' disciples had a difficult time with was loyalty. They enjoyed receiving recognition when the miracles were happening; but when the clouds of the Crucifixion hung over them, they wanted to hide.

6. Being there. Single-again people have often shared with me that the toughest part of their day is coming home from work, knowing no one will be there.

God created us with a burning need to have people in our lives who are significant to us and care for us. This doesn't imply you need a party every day when you come home from work. It does mean that you must have special people in your life who will be there for you when you need them.

Hospital visitation has always felt uncomfortable to me. I feel pretty helpless and realize I can do little to enhance a person's healing process. I pray, encourage, make small talk, smile, and leave. Later, people thank me for the visit. I wonder why. Then they say something like, "Thanks for just being there."

Building relationships helps us discover that there are people who'll love us in times of need.

7. Spiritual resources. Have you ever experienced a period in your life when a crisis hit you full force? I have. The shock and hurt were so great that it seemed my faith in God and His promises had gone on vacation. In times like those, a trusted friend can offer you spiritual resources and strength.

I recently called my friend Jack in the midst of one of my chaos times. I felt reassured to know someone on the other end of the phone, over 2,000 miles away, was listening intently as I shared my struggle. Jack's simple words, "We will have faith for you," were what I needed to hear. I'm not always strong enough to have the faith I need during troubled times. My friends and their spiritual support are invaluable.

Deep relationships with people take on more meaning as we get older. There's a richness in longtime friendships. They give our lives meaning and continuity. Our spiritual growth isn't a solo flight; it's a shared journey.

One of the ongoing struggles that singles face is how much emphasis to place on relationships. A priority for many is finding the ultimate person for them—a potential mate. There's nothing wrong with this unless it becomes a pursuit that prevents other healthy relationships from being built.

I've suggested to many singles across the country that they'd experience less pressure if they formed more brother-sister relationships. Those who feel desperate about finding a mate may assume any interaction you have with the opposite sex is for marriage; don't let that expectation get in your way of building friendships.

Say you are seated in the corner booth at McDonald's, after your midweek singles gathering, with a member of the opposite sex. A few people from your group drift by, greeting you as they pass. The next day, you receive several calls asking if you have something serious going on with the person you were with. You get a little upset, telling the callers you just have a nice friendship with that person.

The truth is, single people need a few platonic friendships with the opposite sex. Many men and women have told me they weren't ready to even consider marriage or involved dating, but they did feel the need to spend time talking with someone other than members of their own sex.

It seems to be human nature in singles groups to want to match people up. Resist the urge. It won't help you, and it certainly won't help the other person.

Friendships that develop within the Christian community should take on the quality of a brother-sister relationship. The actions, conduct, and treatment of your Christian brothers and sisters should parallel that of your family.

Charlie Brown is right when he says he needs all the friends he can get. So do you. Are you developing some good friendships?

Relationship or Rescue Attempt?

Life would be simple in the single-again world if people could recover from their loss, find the right person to share life with, remarry, settle in, and live happily ever after. No trial-and-error relationships. No rejections. No dating games. No hassles. Few people are this fortunate, though. Most reach out and withdraw, get hurt and rejected, promise to go into hiding but continue to extend themselves, knowing that growth always involves risk.

Many divorced and widowed people find themselves in a new relationship and wonder how they got into it, why they're in it, what's going on in it, and how to get out of it. The two greatest questions about human relationships are how to start one and how to end one.

A relationship can end up as a form of rescue for the people involved instead of a healthy remarriage. Are you currently caught in a rescue attempt? I've observed several basic kinds of rescues people engage in when dealing with divorce/death recovery.

Emotional rescue. This involves one person trying to make another person's pain and hurt go away. Our world abounds with codependent care-takers who descend on hurting people. The more horrible your lost-marriage story, the more quickly they find you. Some come spiritually disguised while others come as parent or social worker types. A few might be well meaning, but others have their own agendas.

A few years ago, I listened to the tragic story of a woman in our singles ministry who fortunately survived an emotional-rescue attempt. The male rescuer was handsome, charming, friendly, warm, and deeply spiritual. He chose to dispense his gifts to the hurting woman. After several months of being charmed and apparently delivered from her hurt, the woman discov-ered that her "prince" was really after only one thing—her money. She'd received a large divorce settlement and had given this emotional rescuer several thousand dollars before she finally understood what he really wanted. He wore his disguise well and probably moved on to another struggling person looking for a caretaker.

In my divorce recovery workshops, I fear for the emotionally vulnerable as they tell their tragic tales. I can almost see the emotional rescuers lining up behind their chairs. The tragedy is that when you're emotionally weak, you almost welcome this keeper of hurting souls. A relationship that starts with an offer of help and friendship can soon tangle you up in something far more serious. In effect, it's one sick person attaching to another sick person, not to heal but to force him or her into a dependent relationship.

You may feel you need to be rescued from your pain, hurt, or life situation. Just remember, it won't help you grow and be responsible for yourself. And it could lead to a far more painful relationship than the one just ended.

Relational rescue. This type of rescue is closely akin to emotional rescue. These relationships put a person in your life before you're ready. People who fear loneliness often fall victim to relational rescue. I've listened to them say, "I have always had a man (woman) around and I have to have one now." For them, the "who" is not important. Even someone from Rent-a-Body would do.

The struggle to grow involves confronting yourself without relational scaf-folding. That doesn't suggest you don't need people; it means you refuse to use others to rescue you from life's blank spaces.

Relational rescue can also protect you from having to seriously consider the issue of remarriage. Because your rescuer isn't thinking of moving toward remar-riage, he or she becomes a safe person in your life. People in this situation often cohabit and aimlessly go nowhere. Once that relationship pattern is established, it can be repeated many times after one person or the other moves on.

The end result of relational rescue operations is that people become consumable objects. I call them "throw-away relationships." Some argue that these relationships provide "all the comforts of home" without the legal involvements. According to our legal system, that's no longer true. According to our emotional system, we're lying to ourselves if we say we believe that.

Financial rescue. Divorces cost money, and they start a siphoning process without end. Single parents know that better than most. They struggle to make ends meet with sporadic child support, several jobs, and reduced living standards. As one single mother told me recently, "I just want to find a loving man with good credit and a regular job." Loosely translated, she meant, "I need some financial help."

It's difficult to resist financial aid, even when you can see the strings attached. Some relationships are formed solely for financial reasons. Other needs, attributes, and concerns are overlooked for financial stability. The pressures are understandable, but the results questionable. As one wise person said, "Never sacrifice the future on the altar of the immediate."

Some people cohabit only for financial purposes. Others even marry for the same reasons. The age-old line, "They married for the money," is still in use, only now it's finely disguised.

Of all the rescue attempts that might come your way, the toughest one to resist will be financial. Try to step back long enough to ask hard questions. Some of those questions for second-marriage counseling are:

1. What is the current indebtedness of both parties?
2. Who will be responsible for past debts when they are married?
3. Should there be a prenuptial agreement?
4. What is the current or potential earning power of both parties?
5. What are the financial responsibilities to either spouse's primary family?
6. When you look at all finances honestly, is this marriage affordable, or will it lead to further financial chaos?
7. Are both parties starting out with a solid credit record, or does one party have good credit while the other has little or no credit?
8. Is affordable housing available for this new family?

Try to remember, a second marriage is built on a ladder of love, not dollar signs!

Sexual rescue. Two questions face the single-again person in the sexual area. The first is, "Will I ever have sexual relationships now that I'm no longer married?" The second asks, "Will I practice celibacy during my single-ness and have a sexual relationship again only when I remarry?" Reality requires the sexual issue to be answered, even though most people put it on hold until they're confronted with sexual opportunity.

The common supposition among single-again people is that since you had a sexual relationship within marriage, you should continue to pursue what-ever (or whoever) meets your needs after you're divorced or widowed. For these people, sex becomes a commodity to be sought after, bargained for, and traded as well as feared.

I've listened to many years' worth of Sexual Singles Olympics Games. Often, I'm asked what I think about a situation someone has just related to me. I tell them that what I think isn't important; what matters is how *they* feel and how they live. If you're a Christian, though, what God thinks is most significant.

I've known many people who decided they wouldn't be sexually involved while single again, but then gave in even before their divorces were finalized. They were surprised that it happened, but often allowed it to continue in different relationships.

Love, intimacy, caring, holding, touching, and sexuality are intricately wrapped in the same package. It's hard to sort out what you're after as you struggle through the loss of relationship with a former spouse. When I speak of sexual rescue, I'm not referring to someone who appears at your door wearing his or her "Sexual Rescuer" shirt. Sexual rescue is allowing someone to take you where you aren't sure you want to go. The danger is that once you've been there, it may no longer be a question for you, but an answer. Patterns can form that will lead you to ask, "How did I get here?" How? You led the rescue party!

Parental rescue. "Please, somebody, take these kids off my back!" This was a half-serious, half-joking comment I overheard as a single mother, Ann, hauled her three kids off to the car after a church singles event. Assuming the role of a single parent is one of the toughest post-divorce/death responsi-bilities in the world of the single-again person. After many years of observa-tion, I'm convinced that single parents should all receive the highest award for valor on life's battlefield. The custodial parent often ends up acting as both mother and father to the children. It's an exhausting job, emotionally debilitating, and generally thankless. It's little wonder the worn-out and embattled among single parents cast weary glances over their shoulders, hoping for any form of relief.

There's no unending line of surrogate parental candidates, as most single parents will attest. In fact, most people seem to run away from any challenge in this area. As Andy recently told me, "I want to wear a shirt to our singles functions that says, 'Will date woman with no children.'"

Reasons for dodging surrogate parenthood include not wanting the extra responsibility, and being unwilling to take on another financial burden. Men and women who have children of their own may find it overwhelming to date other single parents.

Parental rescue is a desperate need for some people, but many second marriages only become trade-offs in this area. Most childless people don't want to make the sacrifice of assuming someone else's child-raising responsibilities.

How do you avoid the parental-rescue mindset? *First,* by deciding that you can be the best single parent in history and by learning how to do it. *Second,* by understanding that probably no one, not even a stepparent, will feel the way you do about your children. You, as their parent, have a stronger commitment to them. A stepparent has only an "inherited" commitment to them. That doesn't prohibit effective, dedicated, loving stepparenting. It simply means that the birth parent will always feel differently than the stepparent. Knowing that ahead of time will help you build a smoother parenting structure.

In Judith Wallerstein's excellent book *Second Chances,* only a tiny group of children whose parents had remarried felt their stepparents had been more effective and helpful in their lives than the absent parents. The struggle of a primary parent versus a stepparent will always be part of a second marriage.

There's no rescue from single parenting. A remarriage will provide help, but it can never remove you from the primary parent role that divorce or death placed you in.

Vocational rescue. Vocationally, people have two basic choices after they lose a mate. They can continue an established career or begin a new one. (Or, they can look around for someone to rescue them from having to find a career.)

Divorce and death are major crises. They head every list of life stresses. Our struggle is to make some kind of sense out of them, living through and beyond them toward new life and growth.

A major crisis always gives a person an opportunity to set goals, and review his or her life. Often singles make vocational changes after doing some self-examination. Success often replaces past failures, and new attitudes about personal abilities develop.

For someone who hasn't pursued a vocation over the years (the case for many single-again women), it's easier to look for the vocational security a prospective mate might provide, than to begin a new career. Because of the economic realities in today's world, though, I feel strongly that women as well as men need to have careers they can establish if the need arises.

Dependency rescue. When someone does for us what we choose not to do for ourselves, dependency arises. The struggle in a marital relationship is to develop a form of interdependency between two people. Whether single or married, most people live in one of four modes: dependence, independence, codependence, or interdependence. Take a moment right now and ask yourself where you've lived in your past marriage, where you're living now, and where you'd like to live in any future relationship.

There are many other forms of rescue we haven't discussed here. I've tried to highlight the main forms I've observed in working with people who are thinking about and preparing for possible remarriage. Rescue is an easy way to dodge the bullet of personal responsibility and growth. Many rescuees will grab any rope tossed in their direction, without asking what's attached to the other end. Over the years, I've watched too many rescued people end up back in the sea of singleness. Always take the time to ask yourself hard questions as you prepare mentally and emotionally for whatever lies ahead.

Assessing Personal Growth

1. Write down the three most meaningful relationships in your life right now and what you feel each one contributes to you.
2. What kind of relationship do you feel most in need of?
3. Are you more comfortable with giving or receiving in a relationship?
4. Where do you find your community support?
5. If you have a healthy brother-sister relationship with a member of the opposite sex, how do you feel this helps you?
6. Have you been caught in a relational rescue attempt lately? Describe your experience to your group.

Chapter Five

It's a Jungle Out There

"Human sexuality is a gift from God. It comes with God's imprint —
FRAGILE! HANDLE WITH CARE!"

It was time for questions at the end of a singles seminar. At the back of the room, a hand went up very slowly. As I pointed in that direction, a quavering voice stammered, "Would you s-s-s-ay something about s-s-s- s-ex?" I responded by saying, "Sex is fun!" Several laughed while others remained embarassed and silent. I knew that wasn't the answer the questioner had wanted. My second response was to acknowledge that sex is a genuine problem for many single-again people. The audience breathed more easily and nodded their heads in agreement.

Of all the issues I've been asked by singles to address over the last 20 years, the question of how to handle singleness and sexuality is the most frequent.

Many assume that after a person has been married and has enjoyed a sexual relationship, he or she simply cannot live without sex. After watching a few television soaps, it appears that one of life's great pastimes is playing musical beds. Many of those people jumping in and out are either divorced, about to be divorced, having an affair, or single. If we absorb what we witness on television long enough, we might be convinced that everyone lives that way. The media can brainwash Christians to the point where they move from God's standard to man's.

One Sunday morning, Brooke approached me at the end of our singles class. She stated that she was newly divorced and wanted to know why many of her former spouse's male friends were calling her, asking if she had any "needs" they could help fulfill. (I can't tell you what they really asked.) Her question was, "Why?"

I'm not sure of the answer, but I've heard the same story from many singles.

Sex and Sexuality

We could define sex as a biological function. That's the level at which many people deal with it. On a higher level, though, we must deal with sexuality as a total package. That package doesn't consist of only biology. It includes intimacy, love, feelings, consideration, kindness, caring, support, and trust. Sex involves one's whole emotional being. It is total involvement with another person, and continues that way through life. This isn't easy to come to grips with. Many people never see beyond shortsighted sex to understand the complete view and what it involves.

Is your outlook and understanding of sexuality short-circuited by recognizing only the biological level?

Our society is sex-saturated. Much of today's advertising is tied to sexual identification. You're entirely out of step if you don't follow the stream of today's sexual thinking. Rather than just admitting sex is a big problem and talking about something else, let's explore some of the reasons that people get sexually involved.

1. Loneliness. A few pages back, I talked about this problem. Many singles have shared with me that they became sexually intimate with another person to eliminate their consuming loneliness, at least for one evening. In the deep moments of a sexual relationship, their loneliness seemed to vanish. The problem is that it returned again after the experience ended. The supposed cure was actually only a Band-Aid for the problem.

We all know how good a hug feels when we are hurting. It makes us feel warm, cared for, accepted. A sexual encounter can bring about those same feelings. It can be a way of telling yourself you are okay after all, and that you won't be lonely anymore. But the morning after, you realize that you've only traded some of your loneliness for short-lived affection.

2. Desire to be loved. There is probably no better feeling than knowing that we're deeply loved. I meet many people who are starved for love. They often reach out frantically, searching for any kind of love. In a marriage, everyone experiences some form of love from their mate. That love gives a feeling of security. In the world of the suddenly single, there's often a deep desire to prove that one is lovable, especially after a severe rejection.

There are many ways to feel loved without being sexually involved. The old saying, "Never replace the future on the altar of the immediate," holds true. Many singles go the instant-intimacy route, trying to prove they are lovable.

3. Manipulation and intimidation. "If I don't go to bed with him, he won't ask me out again." I've heard that statement hundreds of times from single women. It sounds like the threat of the hijacker who says to an airplane pilot, "I want $10,000,000 or I'll explode this bomb." It's called intimidation, and our society has become expert at using it. We experience intimidation everywhere. Unions ask for more money and threaten to strike if they don't get it; we threaten to sue our neighbor if his dog doesn't stay off our lawn. We live in a litigation-happy society. In all areas, the message is, "Give me what I want or I'll punish you physically, emotionally, socially, mentally, or financially."

When a person trades a sexual encounter for an evening on the town, fearing there won't be any more dates, she's being manipulated. The tragedy is that this can become a way of life. Sexual bartering is about as prevalent as window shopping.

Victims of the sexual intimidation-manipulation game walk away feeling used and conned. Their feelings are ignored, and their self-esteem is left begging.

4. Sexual rights. I've heard many single-again people say they have a right to a sexual relationship with any consenting adult they choose. As a professor in my college used to say, however, "Your rights extend to the end of your nose." A sexual encounter involves two people. Do the rights of the other person supersede yours, or do yours supersede his or hers?

Your rights and the rights of others are precious and guarded responsibilities. When you use someone else for your own gratification, you violate his or her rights.

5. Self-gratification. We are living in a "me first" decade where you look out for number one, and step on others to fulfill your own needs. You hurt others so that you can be satisfied, and you try to catch the brass ring for yourself. But how long can your needs be met at someone else's expense?

Before long, the other person will feel hurt, used, and will grow increasingly calloused toward you.

Most singles organizations have a problem with a group of wandering singles known as "body snatchers." They are marauders who invade singles groups to satisfy their own sexual needs and experience another conquest.

I asked one woman how she handles being approached by a "body snatcher." "I laugh a lot, look him in the eye, and say, 'You've got to be kidding.' Then I walk away." This is probably the best reaction. And in case women readers are thinking that men are always the marauders, let me tell you, there are many women in the seducing business.

You may be thinking, this sounds like a swinging singles group you might read about in a magazine. My experience has been that these problems exist in church-oriented singles groups everywhere. The only difference is that sexual issues aren't talked about openly in religious groups.

6. Everyone is doing it. We live in an age of conscious moral collapse. We are easily seduced by the thoughts, "Everyone is doing it," "Everyone is buying it," "Everyone is wearing it," and "Everyone is going there." Clothing fads tell us that if we don't buy name-brand apparel, we'll be stared at when we go out. The insinuation is that we'd better get with it or we'll be out of step with the world.

The same mindset carries into the area of sexual involvement. Society says everyone is having sex with everyone else and you're abnormal if you don't participate. There's strong group pressure to conform and not be left at the gate when the race starts. The threat of AIDS and other sexually transmitted diseases hasn't slowed the race very much.

But you can't get your standards from the crowd. They must come from you. Absorbing others' views and standards leaves you unsure about who you are. No one enjoys living with uncertainties. You are your own person, unlike anyone else!

7. I can't live without sex. I often listen to this myth as it passes around singles groups. The logic is that sex drive and sexual fulfillment are human needs that must be met, whether it's inside or outside of marriage. In his book *Do I Have to Be Me?* Dr. Lloyd Ahlem says:

> Some people try to fulfill their love needs sensually and grow no further. When adults preoccupy themselves with physical love, they can fall into the worst type of lust. They exploit the partner physically and emotionally while focusing their fantasy life continually on sex at the animal level. The current hedonistic philosophy suggests that sensual

pleasure is the fulfillment rather than the beginning of a healthy love experience.[1]

I've met many singles who are celibate and have been that way for years. They've made that choice for their single-now status. They aren't strange looking folks with little horns protruding from their ears! They are happy, growing people who've simply exercised their right to choose celibacy and are living out that choice until they remarry.

Several recent magazines have reported a growing interest in celibacy for singles. Maybe we've reached a saturation point in the sexual jungle, and some people are looking for more meaningful ways to handle their sexuality. Doing so isn't easy, but neither is running a marathon. The end result is the important part.

Try to remember that sex was made for man and woman, but man and woman weren't made merely for sex.

Just talking about the reasons why conflict occurs when single-again people face sex doesn't solve the problem. Many single-again people are looking for others to justify their sexual desires. Others are simply trying to decide what to do. As one man recently stated, "Don't tell me to take more cold showers. My water bill is high enough already."

Three Attitudes toward Dealing with the Sexual Struggle

Attitude one. Sex is okay—anytime, any place, with anyone who's a consenting, legal adult. Just make sure you "practice safe sex." Does that sound a little like the last television show you watched? Probably! A large segment of the singles world holds this attitude. They follow the slogan, "If it feels good, do it." When we call this "sexual liberty" or "sexual freedom," we forget that freedom always comes with responsibilities attached. In the world of sexual license, there is seldom thought of responsibility. This is, at best, random sex.

Attitude two. Sex is okay—anytime, any place, with anyone of legal age, but only if you have a "meaningful relationship" with the person. The question that arises here is, "What does meaningful mean?" If I said I had a meaningful breakfast this morning, would you know what I had? It could be two vitamins and a glass of juice, or the whole breakfast special at my neighborhood restaurant. What's known as meaningful to one person may lack significance to another.

In the above context, meaningful could indicate you've had three dates with the same person before you engaged in sex. It could imply 60 dates. It could mean engagement.

Some people would call this "selective sex." Many singles find themselves in this situation. They don't want to be known as "bed hoppers," so they opt for minimal involvement to justify a sexual relationship.

Attitude three. Sex is a gift from God and it comes with great responsibilities to the participants. God has stamped sex with the words, FRAGILE— HANDLE WITH CARE! It is best and enjoyed to its fullest "within the context of a marital relationship." Sounds rather restrictive, doesn't it? You might wonder if anyone in today's world really believes this. Contrary to what you might think, there are many single-again people who believe this attitude is the right one for them and seek to live by it.

These three attitudes are widely scattered throughout the singles community. To sharpen your own focus regarding sexuality, ask yourself these questions:

1. Which of the three attitudes describes your own thinking? Be honest.
2. How did you arrive at that attitude? What led you to it and who or what influenced you?
3. Is it the right place for you to be? Why?
4. Where do you think God wants you to be? Why?

What I've discovered from talking to thousands of single people about this subject is that many of them have never thought much about where they stand. They've developed a conditional position, thinking, "I'll see what happens and what kinds of opportunities come up. Then I'll decide."

Living by situation ethics is always precarious. You never have a solid foundation. You're completely subject to your present emotions. It's as if you're standing on a cloud.

People with thoughtful convictions draw respect. Those who live in the side alleys of life are never taken too seriously.

The above questions will provide you with a lot of homework. If you spend time with these questions, you will find your sexual struggles greatly reduced.

What Does God Think about Sex and Singleness?

That's a good question, yet many people don't want to know the answer. If you've decided to follow God, then you need to understand the implications of that decision.

The Scriptures give a general principle for all our behavior in 1 Corinthians 10:31: "So, whether you eat or drink, or whatever you do, do all to the glory of God." The "whatever" is comprehensive. It includes how we relate to others sexually. Most people would look at the obvious things like fun, hobbies, conversation, and jobs. Paul put the "all" in there for our own safety in making life decisions.

Several years ago, my friend suggested that I always consider two questions when making a decision. The first was, "Can this be done for the glory of God?" The second asked, "Is this the best that God intends for me?" Those two questions might help you arrive at some rapid solutions in dealing with sexual issues.

Paul speaks even more specifically in 1 Corinthians 6:13-20. He starts by talking about food again. (I guess he knew that would get our attention every time):

> "Food is meant for the stomach and the stomach for food"—and God will destroy both one and the other. The body is not meant for immorality, but for the Lord, and the Lord for the body. And God raised the Lord and will also raise us up by His power. Do you not know that your bodies are members of Christ? Shall I therefore take the members of Christ and make them members of a prostitute? Never! Do you not know that he who joins himself to a prostitute becomes one body with her? For, as it is written, "The two shall become one flesh." But he who is united to the Lord becomes one spirit with Him. Shun immorality. Every other sin which a man commits is outside the body; but the immoral man sins against his own body. Do you not know that your body is a temple of the Holy Spirit within you, which you have from God? You are not your own; you were bought with a price, so glorify God in your body."

These are some of the strongest words Paul spoke regarding the use of our bodies. The people in Paul's era faced the same issues and struggles we face today. The only difference between Paul's time and ours is that we get better media coverage!

Single-again Christians usually listen to the logic the world offers about sex. They battle with their own worldly emotions, but still must measure them against what the Scriptures teach. It's only after Scripture is addressed that answers begin to come clear.

A Christian's sexual ethics and conduct should be determined by what God intended when He gave man and woman the gift of sex. This gift was certainly a great idea! Sex was granted for pleasure as well as procreation. But it was also given in trust. This trust was that it would be used within the boundaries God intended. I believe the Scriptures are clear in stating that those limits are only within the framework of marriage.

That doesn't mean that having a sexual relationship outside of marriage isn't fun. It does indicate that extramarital sex will never bring you God's intended best in the way of enjoyment and fulfillment. Perhaps this is why so many sexually worn-out singles ask me if there is another answer they missed along the way.

God knew what He was doing when He designed men and women! It's only when we try to do the redesigning that we get into trouble. Getting mad at God, and doing your own thing because you dislike His design, won't bring you happiness.

Sex is a choice, and choices always bring responsibility. As a single-again person, you won't be around too long before you're confronted with the sexual issue. You may begin rationalizing before you even have a chance to check into God's purposes. Your own needs, desires, feelings, frustrations, and lack of love may dominate your thinking. Let me share several suggestions for working through this issue.

1. Find what the Scriptures teach about sex. Read the references and commentaries.
2. Read a few good books that cover, in-depth, the areas of sexuality, singleness, and marriage.
3. Talk to God about it. He promises to help you through your struggles. Tell God how you feel, and where you need help.
4. Learn to share your feelings and struggles with other single Christians. Ask them what they do, and what answers they've found. Don't push the topic under the rug in your singles group. Talk it out.
5. Don't club other people with your sexual convictions. Instead, try saying, "I've found this to be the best way for me to live." Leave others free to live as they choose. All you can do is share where you are, and how you arrived there.
6. Make sure your sexual standards and conditions don't come from the media.

At the start of this chapter, I said this was a tough area. You won't resolve it in the next three minutes. Even after you do resolve it for yourself, you will still struggle with it. But rest assured, you are not alone. *God cares!*

Assessing Personal Growth

1. What's the biggest problem for you in dealing with your sexuality as a single-again person?
2. Which of the three attitudes toward sex describes you? Why?

3. Why do you believe sexuality and singleness are seldom discussed in church-related singles groups?
4. Do you feel free to tell your date about your sexual standards?
5. What sexual problems are you struggling with, and what are you doing to resolve them?

Chapter Six

Get Going, Get Growing

*"The Wind of God is always blowing,
but you must first hoist your sails."*

Francis Fénelon

For the person who is suddenly single again there are five major building blocks of growth. All deal with change and bring big adjustments into your new life. These building blocks address the personal, social, vocational, sexual, and spiritual areas of life. In this chapter, we want to take a closer look at the spiritual side.

The death or divorce of a mate can profoundly affect a person's spiritual growth. Some who aren't spiritually oriented prior to the crisis develop faith as a result of it. Others who were connected can become spiritually stagnant, separated from God. Still others get mad at God and blame Him for allowing their tragedy to occur.

One of my goals is to help you examine your life and growth as a single-again person. A primary key to your development is spiritual.

What Is Spiritual Growth?

The Bible speaks a lot about growing. Writing to the early Church in Ephesus, Paul says, "Rather, speaking the truth in love, we are to grow up in every way into Him who is the head, into Christ" (Eph. 4:15).

51

Peter tells us to "grow in the grace and knowledge of our Lord and Savior Jesus Christ" (2 Peter 3:18). In his first letter, he states, "So put away all malice and all guile and insincerity and envy and all slander. Like newborn babes, long for the pure spiritual milk, that by it you may grow up to salvation" (1 Peter 2:1-2).

In His earthly ministry, Jesus repeatedly talked of growth, and used many agrarian examples to illustrate His points. He spoke of planting seeds, growing wheat, and harvesting crops.

A crisis can either deter our growth or cause us to mature more than ever. We decide which it will be. In his letter to the Romans, Paul says, "And we know that all things work together for good to them that love God, to them who are the called according to His purpose" (Rom. 8:28, KJV). This verse does not say that everything that happens to us is enjoyable. It affirms that God will work everything together so that the end result is good.

Losing a mate isn't usually regarded as a good thing. But God can bring value and cause tremendous growth in your life from that loss. Let's look at how this can happen.

Spiritual growth is believing God's promises. We build trust with God the same way we acquire trust with other human beings. Trust grows when it's put to the test. Our muscles develop only when they're challenged, not when they lie dormant. I'm always amazed when people tell me they've been shocked when God answered their prayers. That's strange. God promised He'd answer if we asked. Sometimes, we have to find renewed faith in God first by trusting Him with the little things, then giving Him bigger ones. He wants us to claim His promises, not just memorize them!

Spiritual growth is removing fears from your life. I'll talk more about fear in another chapter. So let me just mention one of God's assurances about fear. In 2 Timothy 1:7, the writer says, "For God hath not given us the spirit of fear; but of power, and of love, and of a sound mind" (KJV). One measure of spiritual growth is to stack up your fears alongside God's promises. You'll find that God has the bigger pile every time.

Spiritual growth is having your hurts healed. As a little boy, I would run to my mother after I'd fallen and scraped my knee. Mom never yelled, saying I should watch more carefully where I was going. She simply bent down, cleaned the cut, and applied a good dose of iodine. As she bandaged the cut, I was never sure whether the iodine hurt more than the wound itself. She patted me on the head and sent me back to play. The hurt subsided in a few minutes. The Band-Aid stayed for a few days, but the scar from the wound remained forever. You should see my knees!

Healing takes place in our lives when we stop calling attention to our wounds, and allow scar tissue to cover them. In the words of Dr. Robert Schuller, "We must turn our scars into stars." James tells us, "Therefore confess your sins to one another, and pray for one another, that you may be healed. The prayer of a righteous man has great power in its effects" (James 5:16).

Some healing will take place in newly formed Christian friendships and support groups. Author Henri Nouwen says,

A Christian Community is therefore a healing community not because wounds and pains are alleviated, but because wounds and pains become openings or occasion for a new vision. Mutual confession then becomes a mutual deepening of hope and sharing weakness becomes a reminder to one and all of the coming strength.[1]

The healing of our hurts is a sign of spiritual growth. Healing takes place in the emotional, psychological, and physical areas of our lives. Often, it must start from the inside out because many of our wounds are within. Internal bleeding is always the most difficult to stop. That's why we must turn to God, our true physician!

Spiritual growth is coming home. Some years ago, I became hooked on a few lines from a song by Chuck Girard. The tune was called "Welcome Back," and it said, "Welcome back to the things that you once believed in. Welcome back to what you knew was right from the start."[2] I meet many single-again people who are coming home to God through their crisis, being "welcomed back."

Loss is not a place to hide, but a situation to grow through. God can use your experience to bring you back to a point of spiritual growth.

Spiritual growth is building or rebuilding your relationship with God. In his book *No Longer Strangers,* Bruce Larson says:

A right relationship means that one has heard the good news that God says to us in Jesus Christ: "I love you as you are. I love you unconditionally. I have already given Myself to you totally, and now all I ask is that you begin to respond to My love and My commitment to you by committing to Me all of yourself that you are able to give."[3]

That's the beginning of building a connection with God. As in earthly relationships, there must be a maintenance program if the relationship is to grow. I meet Christians every day who have had a vital encounter with God. At one time, they joined God's family. They entered the race; they just never traveled very far from the starting line. Then chaos, problems, and life struggles invaded. The question, "Why me?" came up. Most often the answer was, "I don't know!" Perhaps a better question is, however, "How can I grow through this time and come out better because of it?"

Building is beginning a relationship with God. You may need to start your life right there. Rebuilding is coming back to God, and continuing the growth you once began.

Spiritual growth is coming alive! Can you remember a moment when you felt full of life? It wasn't just because your heart was beating, or because something good had happened to you. It was a special experience that was hard to describe in human language. But you knew you were alive, and you savored that moment.

Those are the mountaintops of life. For some of us, it may seem as if the valleys outnumber the peaks by a hundred to one. Spiritual growth is sensing that you're completely alive, centered in God's love.

John Powell, author of *Fully Human, Fully Alive*,[4] says there are five things that contribute to one's sense of being fully alive. They are: 1) to accept oneself; 2) to be oneself; 3) to forget oneself in loving; 4) to believe; 5) to belong. To these five I would add one of my own: To minister to others and to be ministered to.

Take a minute to use those six principles as a checklist, or a spiritual pulse-taking. Be honest. If you score low in certain areas, this is where you need to concentrate some of your growth efforts.

Jesus said in John 10:10, "I came that they might have life, and have it abundantly." That sounds to me like being alive! For you, it might mean shaking the trappings of another life, and deciding to get your new one growing! All spiritual development is measured by daily discipline. That exercise is never easy.

It's like dieting. The first hour is the hardest. The first day is torture. The first week is agony! Then, all of a sudden, you get in the groove, build up your resistance, and keep going. The results come slowly at first, then more noticeably. You feel excitement as you see the changes.

Then someone throws a pothole in your path—a seven-layer Bavarian chocolate cake, your favorite! Do you taste the frosting just to see what you were delivered from? Do you have a tiny piece so the cake buyer won't feel offended? Do you eat the whole thing because you deserve a reward for not eating cake in the past eight weeks? We all know that kind of experience—"a tangible temptation of the tastiest variety." It's also a turning point, a place to really measure your growth in dieting.

Steps to Spiritual Growth

You'll hit some potholes while growing spiritually. As you come alive, you'll be able to handle them with more skill each time they confront you.

I became a Christian when I was about 12 years old. I remember that my Sunday School teacher and pastor placed more importance on the things I shouldn't do now that I belonged to God, than on the things I should do. My list of negatives grew long and dangerous. It wasn't until many years later that I realized there was another list—shorter and, for the most part, a lot harder. That list contains things that really help a person grow in his relationship with God. I want to share them with you.

1. Prayer. I know we're starting with one of the hardest ones! No wonder the disciples came to Jesus and said, "Lord, teach us to pray" (Luke 11:1). It's difficult to tell whether they wanted to learn for their own reasons, or to identify more closely with Jesus. What's implied in their request, though, is that it's a learned process.

Jesus responded with what is known as the Lord's Prayer. It wasn't meant to be the only prayer, but to be an example, because it sums up what God wants for us. The Lord's Prayer is bare bones, direct communication prayer. It focuses on the practical rather than theological. Scripture doesn't say how often the disciples were to pray it. Jesus simply gave the model, and the disciples went from there.

Prayer, simply defined, is a conversation with God about anything. It is telling God the truth about everything. Prayer is also listening to God. He can speak to us and direct us only if we're quiet long enough to hear His voice. A good rule is to talk 20 percent and listen 80 percent.

All of the elements that build earthly relationships also apply to developing a relationship with God in prayer. You have to talk to Him—in twentieth-century English, or whatever language you speak. Are you communicating with God these days? Are you asking for His help in all of your struggles? Do you have some problems you feel are too big for God, others that you feel God wouldn't be interested in hearing about? Matthew's Gospel puts it this way: "Ask, and it will be given you; seek, and you will find; knock, and it shall be opened to you. For every one who asks receives, and he who seeks finds, and to him who knocks it will be opened "(Matt. 7:7-8).

That's one of God's promises, but we have to do the asking. Prayer is a discipline. It takes time and it takes effort. It is the foundation of a growing faith.

2. Bible study. Four singles crowded into my office. They were excited about the prospect of having a Bible study. We talked about dates, times, and my availability to teach. After we had agreed on these, they turned to go. I stopped them, giving a homework assignment that would prepare them for our next study. Their look of disbelief told me what I already suspected. They wanted me to study the Bible for them, and ladle out the truth for an hour while they listened and then went home.

Real Bible study involves you doing some work—not your preacher or your teacher, but *you*.

Christian bookstores are loaded with study guides, tapes, workbooks, lesson materials, resources, and commentaries. If you are serious about your own growth, you'll need to buy several of these tools and study them for yourself.

That doesn't mean you can't go to a study someone else teaches. But it does mean you can't depend on that as your only study. Just sitting in a room with 10 people, reading a segment of Scripture, and then asking what each one thinks is merely pooling ignorance unless you've done your homework. In order to grow, you have to work!

Second Timothy 2:15 says, "Do your best to present yourself to God as one approved, a workman who has no need to be ashamed, rightly handling the word of truth." These were Paul's words to Timothy as he struggled to grow.

Are you studying? Do you have the materials you need? Are you in a study group that demands something from you, or are you just being spoon-fed? Remember this above all else: you are responsible for your own spiritual growth!

3. Involvement in ministry. Over the last 20 years, I've watched many singles come to a meeting for the first time. They are nervous and unsure about the people, the program, the place, and even themselves. Many come only once, then drift on to some other place. I have discovered that what brings most people back for a second or third time is a reason for them to be there. The best one I've found is holding people responsible for something. I have asked more singles to serve coffee than there are coffeepots in California! Many coffee servers become wonderful group presidents, social chairmen, and retreat leaders.

The beginning of ministry involvement isn't as glorious as we'd like to think.

Jesus' first request to some potential disciples was simply "Follow me"

(Matt. 4:19). That doesn't sound too prestigious. All ministries begin with the followers' involvement. As the followers become more involved and equipped, the tasks become greater and the ministry grows.

I've learned that most people support only what they have a part in creating. Looking for a place to belong is one thing, but having a reason to belong is another. Jesus slowly included the disciples in what He was doing. You need to follow that example, and get involved gradually in ministries. Your desire might be to jump in and take all the reins. Start with one. That will give you a reason to be there. Ministry involvement can range from participating in a small singles' group to serving in a larger church body, from involvement in mission task forces to even serving as an elder or deacon. There are hundreds of opportunities to serve. You just need to start.

4. Fellowship. As a child, I thought fellowship was food and drink in the church hall after a meeting. No one explained to me that fellowship is a lot more than that. It's sharing your life with a supportive community that loves you. Fellowship means revealing the deep truths of your life to others, and accepting the deep truths they share with you.

Sometimes, after finishing a six-week divorce recovery workshop, participants ask if they can continue to meet week after week. When told the seminar is over, they usually respond by saying, "I need these people. They have become my friends. I need their support and fellowship." This kind of fellowship comes from people who share similar struggles and experiences.

Fellowship reminds you that are not alone. It involves having hands that applaud you when you accomplish something, and having hands to catch you when you fall. It means having your own private cheerleading squad. There's a quiet warmth that comes from deep fellowship with other people. It's almost unexplainable, but you certainly know when it's there.

The Christian single-again person is first in fellowship with Christ. That fellowship then extends to every other member of God's family.

5. The witness of your life. Paul was standing before King Agrippa. His life was in peril and he was speaking in his own defense. Paul's only defense was his life and what had happened to him. He was so convincing that when he concluded, Agrippa said, "In a short time you will persuade me to become a Christian" (see Acts 26:28, KJV). Paul wasn't oratorical. He wasn't overwhelming. He wasn't overly spiritual. Paul simply told the story of his conversion and life afterward.

The strongest witness anyone can give is to put his or her life on public display. Sharing your faith is a big part of spiritual growth. Witnessing is taking others behind the scenes, allowing them to see what God is doing and has done in your life.

As I was finishing a singles conference on the East Coast some years ago, a strange thought popped into my head. A tape in my mind seemed to keep replaying the words, "So what?" I concluded the session by saying, "After all that was said and shared here, I want to close with a question, *So what?*"

That's what I'm asking you now: So what??? What about your spiritual growth? Do you care enough to take some time right now and do a spiritual self-evaluation? No one else can do it for you. Here are some suggestions to help:

1. Take an honest look at where you are in your spiritual life and where you'd like to be.
2. Make some positive growth plans. Write them down. Put them on your calendar.
3. Be willing to share with others how you're doing and to ask their help if you need it.
4. Don't be afraid to take risks and make new commitments to grow.
5. Discover what spiritual gifts you have and find a way to use them.
6. Learn to feed yourself spiritually.
7. Watch out for people who set themselves up as spiritual gurus.
8. Don't let others dictate your growth patterns.

Spiritual growth is not a race, it's a journey. Although you don't need to be more "spiritual" than someone else, no matter where you are in your spiritual growth, you'll need to be accountable to someone, you'll need to practice your spiritual disciplines, and you'll need to develop a weekly plan for your spiritual growth. If you fail to do your own homework, you will never reach spiritual maturity.

My prayer for you is that as a suddenly single-again person, you are seeking spiritual growth.

Assessing Personal Growth

1. Write down one area in your spiritual growth that you feel good about.
2. What spiritual growth areas are you struggling with?
3. Name one thing that has profoundly affected your spiritual growth in the past year.
4. How have you changed as a result of spiritual growth?
5. Who has helped you the most in your spiritual growth, and how has he or she done so?

Chapter Seven

If Happiness Is Being Single, Why Do These People Look So Sad?

"Happiness is an inside job."

John Powell

The sleek Corvette jetted past me on the freeway. As it disappeared from view, I noticed that its license-plate holder bore the slogan, "Happiness is being single." I see that motto often. Sometimes it's on plain old economy cars, other times on sportier models. Occasionally, I try to catch a glimpse of the drivers. I want to see if they look happy, and I want to know if that happiness is somehow connected to their singleness.

In speaking to singles audiences over the years, I've had the opportunity to look into the faces of many singles who wish they were someplace else. Their expressions say, "Singleness is the pits."

Many have approached me after a meeting to say they didn't want to be there, but a friend had literally yanked them from their hiding places and dragged them along.

Happiness usually isn't going to your first-ever singles meeting as a single-again adult. Happiness is not often dispensed at the door as you enter a singles function. Many newly single people expect those functions to provide them with an instant supply of happiness. Their message seems to be, "I'm not very happy, so make me happy!"

Wherever you go, happiness is something you bring with you. You can't just go looking for it. You won't find someone who can hand it to you. As Christin left our Tuesday night meeting, she smiled at me and said she was leaving early because there weren't any men there she was interested in. That was not the first time I'd heard that kind of comment. What the woman was really saying was that she wanted to find someone to make her happy, and she'd quickly disqualified those at the meeting.

Is happiness a place? Is it a person? Is unhappiness being in the wrong place? Is it being with the wrong person? People and places do contribute to our emotions. But they are so conditional and variable that they can't be a true source of happiness.

Happiness Hooks

In my work with singles, I hear certain phrases I call "happiness hooks," which give the impression that happiness hinges on the occurrence of one thing. Let's examine some of those hooks.

If I could just have . . . Mark Twain once said, "If a person had the whole world, he would still want the moon fenced in to shine on his potato patch." What he was saying is that there's no end to wanting. Commercial advertising says the same thing. When the automobile was invented and became marketable, the goal was to put one in every garage in America. Several decades later, one car isn't enough for a family. Now we need one per person. We cry, "If I could just have a new one, a better one, a more expensive one, a more sophisticated one." Acquisitions are rungs on our ladder of success. Society says we always need more! Consequently, we've become consumed with getting. It's little wonder that we believe happiness comes from obtaining just one more thing.

Singles are often led to believe their happiness would be complete if they could just meet that certain person. Many married people feel they'd be happier if they were married to someone else. So they leave one person in exchange for another. And unhappiness gets easily traded for divorce. The high failure rate of second marriages proves that happiness is not always found in other people. Most often, one set of problems simply gets exchanged for another.

Scores of searching singles float in and out of singles meetings looking for someone to make them happy. How would you like the ominous responsibility of trying to make someone happy? We all contribute to other people's happiness, but we aren't the source of it. I meet many divorced and widowed people who feel that the happiness they once knew disappeared with their former spouse. They have decided they'll never be happy again as a single person, and that any future form of happiness is contingent upon finding a person to marry.

I saw this illustrated again recently by a young man who came to my office. As he shared about how he'd grown, I noted that his life was moving along pretty well. The man had experienced a divorce a few years back, but had worked hard to rebuild his life from the wreckage. His parting comment surprised me, "Now if I could just find the right woman to marry, I'd be complete."

Was the young man suggesting he was deficient because he wasn't remarried? Many singles I talk with appear to feel this way. Any happiness in their lives seems to hinge on finding someone to complete them. But God never said that one was an unhappy number! Being a part of two doesn't necessarily guarantee happiness in anyone's life.

If I could just be . . . When I was 12, I wanted to be 13 so that I would be a teenager. When I was 13, I wanted to be 16 so that I could get my driver's license. When I was 16, I wanted to be 18 so that I could be out of high school. When I was 18, I wanted to be 20 so that I would be an adult. When I was 21, I wanted to be 25 so that my insurance rates would be lower. What a way to go from 12 to 25!

Have you ever based your happiness on being something else? Perhaps you wanted to be younger, older, wiser, richer, thinner, or fatter. Your list could go on indefinitely. The assumption is that we'd all be happier if we could just be something that lies beyond our grasp.

There's a lot of pretense in the world of the newly single. Many singles gatherings are filled with people trying to be something they are not. Their assumption is, "You will accept me only if I paint a glowing picture of myself and impress you. If I can gain your acceptance, I will be happy and perhaps you will be happy, too." From time to time, we all meet people who are playing, "Let's pretend." This is an enormous problem, particularly for new singles.

I have often felt we should give out buttons at the doors to singles meetings that say, *Be yourself!* We all feel most comfortable when we have the freedom to be who we really are. Wishing you were something you are not prevents you from being happy about who you are. Deceiving others only locks you into living out a hopeless lie.

Becoming single again doesn't change who you are on the inside. Singles who live from the inside out are freer to experience what real happiness is.

If only someone would . . . love me, marry me, make all my troubles go away, make me happy. Many of us would like to rent someone for a day who could do all those things. Some singles search for their own private "answer person" who can do it all for them. Stop looking! Even if you found one, he or she would only smother you.

Death and divorce bring an endless chain of complications into a person's life. Since you're human, you'll have a few days when you wish a knight in shining armor would stop at your house and take care of everything. The reality is, however, that you will have to do most, if not all, of your own work. You'll have days when you feel as if the gravel of life has been dumped in your living room. It's tempting to go looking for someone with a dump truck, who'll haul away all that gravel for you.

I can recall a beleaguered single mother, Mary, who sat in my office. She had too many bills to pay, too few hours at home with her children, too many repairs needing attention, and too little money to make ends meet. Mary's parting comment was, "I'm so tired and overloaded. I just wish I could find some guy with good credit and a steady job to marry me. I'm too worn out to keep going at it alone."

I probably hear that kind of remark at least twice a week in my counseling. "If only someone would rescue me from all my chaos." It's a valid feeling.

I would be a lot happier if . . . Almost anything could be written after that kind of statement. Most people, single or married, feel that happiness is "out there" somewhere, just waiting to be tapped or trapped. It becomes the elusive butterfly that lingers just beyond our reach. The problem with this "iffy" happiness is that we're dealing with the unknown. There are no guarantees that we'd be any happier than we are now, even if we had everything we've ever dreamed of.

In Luke 18, there is an account of a rich young ruler who seemed to have it all. From his conversation with Jesus, it was apparent that ultimate happiness still evaded him. He had done everything right, yet there was a vacuum in his life. Jesus' response to his query in verse 22 was to sell all that he had, and distribute the profits to the poor. In doing so, he would possess a real treasure, eternal life. We're told that this young man went away sad, for he had too much to give up. He didn't understand Jesus' statement that true happiness comes not from getting but from giving.

All of us become immersed with acquiring. Often, obtaining people and things becomes our freeway to success and happiness. The problem is that real happiness doesn't come from without; *it comes from within*. Jesus knew that when He tried to unlock the rich young ruler's heart. The scriptural principle is that genuine happiness doesn't come from being either single or married. It comes from within, as we give ourselves to others. It happens when we help hang a rainbow over someone else's storms.

Dr. Maxwell Maltz, author of *Psycho-Cybernetics,* states that "happiness is internal, produced by ideas, thoughts, and attitudes that can be developed and constructed by an individual's own activities." [1] If what Maltz says is true, then I have to assume personal responsibility for my own happiness. It's centered in my inner being and springs from that to everyday living. I have to look for the source of happiness rather than its manifestations. When I talk with singles about finding happiness, I make the following suggestions.

Four Keys to Happiness

Put the Creator at the center. Knowing God and experiencing real happiness go hand in hand. Having God as the center and source of your happiness means that you don't have to rely on external forms of happiness to complete your life. No matter how things go on the outside, there will be serenity and trust on the inside.

I meet many single-again people across America who've had little religious orientation. Some of them ask me how God can be the focus and cause of their inner happiness. The answer is simple: By invitation. Bringing God into the center of your life happens when you ask Him to take charge of your life and become that inner source of happiness that will not change, regardless of external situations.

The Scriptures tell us, "Therefore, if any one is in Christ, he is a new creation; the old has passed away, behold, the new has come" (2 Cor. 5:17). Christ at the center of a person's life is the only key to true happiness. He enables you to live with quiet confidence, knowing that Someone other than yourself is in control of your life. Happiness is realizing that the Creator is in charge!

If you have never asked Christ to become your personal Savior, you can do that right now by praying this simple prayer:

> Lord, I recognize that I am a sinner and only You can save me. At this moment, I invite You into my heart and ask You to become Lord and Master of my life from now on. Thank You, Lord, for loving me! Amen.

Don't try to go it alone with God! Another key to happiness is sharing your life with others who also know God as their source of happiness. That doesn't suggest you grab your group of Christian friends and head for the hills to start a commune. It means that you live your life in the marketplace, but draw special strength from your community of Christian friends. The Bible states that "none of us lives to himself" (Rom. 14:7). We draw courage from these concentric circles of relationships that focus on God.

Happiness is being with people who share your faith as well as your struggles. Many of the single-again people I meet are trying to go it alone. They take pride in the fact that they are resourceful, and feel that God plus themselves is all the majority they need in life. This certainly was not Jesus' approach. He was a person for others, and those others helped give meaning to His existence on earth. Jesus wrapped His life in significant relationships with the people around Him.

Do the people around you add to your happiness or detract from it? I said earlier that it isn't someone else's job to make you happy. But, those around you who are happy will make valuable contributions to your growing happiness.

Give yourself away! A third key to happiness is found in giving yourself away to people who need you. Over the years, I've watched many hurting people who are newly single come into a singles group for the first time. They are often a collection of emotional bruises and battle scars. Many are "out of gas." Some just sit, stare, and wonder about this Singles Wasteland they have fallen into.

After a few months, some of the hurts begin to heal and signs of new life appear. As the healing progresses, I find many of these people looking for other hurting people whom they can help. Part of recovery involves helping to restore another person to life. Being a people-helper, however, isn't always easy. Some people will use you in the process. Some will never say thank you, while others will question your motives. Sometimes those who reach out can come home at the end of the day feeling like a garbage collector. Many times it's easier to receive help than to give it.

Recently, at the end of a seminar, Elaine approached me, teary-eyed. She commented on how much help she'd received over the past six weeks from the seminar's small-group experiences. My thoughts went back to the first night this group got together, and the apparent distrust they felt for one another. Now, six weeks later, they had laughed, cried, and struggled together through many of their problems. They had invested in each other's lives, and experienced the happiness and satisfaction that comes from giving yourself away.

Anyone involved in people-helping professions will tell you how tiring, yet rewarding, caring can be. The satisfaction of helping another person deepens your own well of happiness.

Today, there are effective singles groups in thousands of churches across America. Most sponsor Divorce Support and Grief Groups. Make some phone calls in your area and find a group where you can get involved in both receiving and giving yourself away. You can also call N.S.L. (National Association of Single Adult Leaders) at (616) 957-9377 or S.A.M. (Single Adult Ministry) at (719) 635-6020 for the group nearest you!

Learn how to feel good about yourself. A final key to happiness is learning to feel good about yourself. Some time ago, a television commercial featured a group of young people promoting a soft drink. They were depicted romping down a city street singing the words, "Feeling good about yourself!" The implication was, of course, that you'd feel better about yourself if you drank what they were advertising. We all know, however, that happiness isn't found in a bottle, whether it contains soda or alcohol.

Feeling good about yourself will greatly enhance your happiness. Personal happiness is contagious. On the other side, feeling bad about yourself will send others scurrying from your path. Happy people attract happy people. There are several positive things you can do to improve your state of happiness.

1. Be good to yourself. As I stated earlier, I have a friend whose favorite farewell to me is, "Be good to yourself." Usually, I have a hard time with that. It sounds too much like self-indulgence. It's easier for me to give to others, rather than to myself. But my friend has a point. If you are good to yourself, it makes it that much easier to give to others.

In a workshop session, Michelle shared how she'd given herself a trip to Hawaii when told she should be good to herself. Brad, a young man in the same workshop, sent a dozen roses to himself at his office. He said he smiled knowingly to himself while everyone at his office speculated where the roses came from.

Single parents often find themselves giving everything to their children because they feel guilty about the divorce. Children, being who they are, just keep on taking, often giving little in return. Single parents need to monitor the giving to make sure they also give to themselves.

One fast-food specialist has told us for years, "We deserve a break today!" Apparently, too few of us really believe that.

If God's attitude toward humans is to give us good things, I think He would be pleased if we were good to ourselves once in a while.

What one thing can you do to be good to yourself in the next week, month, year?

2. Redecorate and renew your body! Newspaper and magazine ads tell us it's time to shape up. We all wish we could achieve those end results of shaping up that these ads depict, but it sounds too exhausting to think seriously about following through. We make ourselves a "someday" promise. But I've discovered that the self-worth that comes from exercising is worth the time and effort invested. Every time I finish running a few miles, I'm rewarded with a feeling of accomplishment and the knowledge that this is a gift to my body.

How long has it been since you played a sport? Rode a bicycle? Ran a mile? Don't let your excuse be age or lack of condition. In a recent Boston Marathon, the oldest to cross the finish line was well into his 80s!

As you renew your body physically, redecorate your wardrobe as well. The simple act of buying some new clothes can add to your feelings of self-confidence and self-worth. I realize, as you surely do, that an image change may not be an inside change, but it will add greatly to how you feel about yourself.

When was the last time you bought some clothes you liked and enjoyed wearing?

3. Set some achievable goals for yourself! There is no better feeling in all the world than setting a goal and attaining it. It may be running your first marathon or going back to school for that postponed degree. It could involve changing jobs, getting your social life in order, or starting that long overdue diet.

The problem for most of us in setting goals is that we want instant fulfillment. We grow impatient with slowly working toward our goals.

One woman summed up the warm inner feelings of self-accomplishment. "I'm on my own and I made it," she said proudly, waving her new master's degree in my face.

Don't set impossible goals. Set some short-term ones, some mid-term ones, and some long-term ones. Daily, weekly, and monthly goals are the best to start with. Write them down and cross them off your list when attained. Celebrate reaching them with your friends. Get excited about your accomplishments!

What one goal are you working toward right now? What kind of progress are you making? What are your deadlines for reaching that goal? When you achieve your goal, will you be ready to set even higher ones for yourself?

4. Live in anticipation of what God will do in your life. I have a little sign on my desk that says, *God is up to something!* Some who notice it ask me what I think God is up to. I usually respond by saying, "A million different things in a million different lives." The problem is that God doesn't tell us ahead of time. We live anticipating His surprises. That's what makes life exciting. You never quite know what will happen when you give one day at a time to God. He can fill it with challenges that stretch you, or serendipities that fill your cup of happiness.

In Philippians 1:6 Paul says, "For I am confident of this very thing, that He who began a good work in you will perfect it until the day of Jesus Christ" (paraphrase of KJV). This literally means that God will keep on working in your life, regardless of the circumstances and situations you are going through.

One of America's great writers, Nathaniel Hawthorne, summed up happiness in this way: "Happiness is a butterfly which, when pursued, is always just beyond your grasp, but which, if you will sit down quietly, may alight upon you."

Hawthorne was saying that the harder we try to attain happiness, the more it evades us. If we sit still long enough, we will give it a chance to catch up with us. What does happiness mean to you? Take a few moments and think through your response. Are you chasing a dream or working on a reality?

Assessing Personal Growth

1. When you think of a happy single-again person, who comes to mind? Why?

2. What one thing would contribute most to your happiness as a single person?

3. Of all the things I have listed in this chapter to help you feel good about yourself, which one is easiest for you to implement? Which one is hardest?

4. When are you usually the happiest?

5. Is happiness, for you, being single?

Chapter Eight

Unlocking
the Fear Syndrome

"No fear is bigger than God's power to conquer it."

S tacey approached me as the retreat I was conducting came to an
end. She told me she was considering a move from the Midwest to
California. As we talked about the excitement of living in California,
I noticed her expression change from anticipation to fear. Finally, Stacey
admitted she'd like to move but was afraid of such a big change. I asked her
to verbalize her fears. She seemed to put all her anxiety into one bag stating,
"I'm afraid I won't make it out there!"

I asked her what would happen if she didn't make it and had to return to
her present community. She responded by saying that everyone in town
would know she had failed.

Stacey feared it all—new circumstances, the possibility of failure, even
what others might think.

These are all common fears that cross the landscape of our lives. We give
them so much power that they often immobilize us, keeping us from positive
action and growth.

A single-again person often gets caught between two worlds. One is the
world of past failures; the other is the world of possible failures. Both can

suffocate us when it's time to make an important decision. Sometimes we think it's easier not to make a decision at all for fear of making the wrong one.

Recently, I asked a group of singles to list the things they feared most. Their responses didn't include snakes, spiders, bugs, and assorted members of the opposite sex. They feared things such as being alone, being unsuccessful, failure, rejection, marrying and not marrying, being hurt, finances, terminal illness, losing a career through corporate downsizing, and what others think.

If you spend any time reading your daily newspaper or watching the evening news, you'll quickly conclude that the world is filled with fearful things. We walk down a street after dark and are filled with anxiety when we hear footsteps approaching from behind. We leave the supermarket late at night and double-check to make sure no one is hanging around the parking lot. Crowded self-defense classes around the country teach people how to protect themselves from attackers. Men fear being mugged and robbed. Women fear rape. We all dread nuclear annihilation and economic chaos, along with earthquakes, floods, fires, and assorted natural disasters. We have become a fearful society.

Somehow, the outer fears in life seem easier to handle. We can see them, identify them, and respond to them. However, it's the inner fears that become realities. Let's take a closer look at some of the worries that invade our lives.

Fear of Being Unsuccessful

Every young baseball player dreams of hitting a home run, with bases loaded in the bottom of the ninth inning, and his team losing by three runs. That same dream can turn to ashes if he strikes out, though. So how does he avoid that failure? By not going to bat or playing baseball. Then he will never have the problem of striking out—but neither will he have the joy of hitting a home run!

Every decision in life contains the dynamic tension of failure or success. We envy the winners, but no one wants to identify too closely with the losers.

Many single-again people find themselves locked out of success and achievement because their lives are clouded by past failures. You can't change past failures into successes, but you can learn from them. Yesterday's defeats should never hamper today's attempts.

A number of years ago, I saw a little sign that explains why some people never reach out for new challenges. The words posted were, *Somebody said it couldn't be done, so I didn't even try!*

There will always be voices telling you to sit on the sidelines. It's a good thing for you and me that Alexander Graham Bell, Thomas Edison, Henry Ford, and many others tuned out the voices of discouragement in their lives. If you have those voices around you, buy a set of earplugs.

Fear of Failure

This fear is closely similar to the fear of being unsuccessful. At one time in my own life, fear of failure kept me out of many new ventures. It was only when I learned I had the freedom to fail that I began to deal with my fears. As a young Christian, I was taught that I should never fail at anything. Christians were always winners! Then I began to notice that the Bible was full of accounts about leaders who didn't always succeed at what they attempted. Somehow, God still had a great love for and patience with those leaders. He kept encouraging and cheering them on. He didn't brand them as failures and move on to those with greater possibilities. Just a look at the 12 disciples' lives and struggles would hearten most of us.

Peter's adventure of walking on water demonstrates the kind of faith it takes to step out of the boat. It also illustrates what it's like not only to walk on the water but to also sink into it. This incident helped Peter learn to risk both success and failure in his growing process.

Are people who try things without succeeding considered failures? I don't believe they are. Even though our society often rewards winners and penalizes losers, Jesus encouraged people who tried and failed! He affirmed them! He loved them! He didn't see only what people were; He also saw what they could become with His help. At first, Peter failed in his water-walking adventure. But Jesus' words lifted Peter, saving him from nearly drowning.

What would you attempt to do if you knew it was okay to fail? What is keeping you from trying?

I've listened to people tell me that many singles are losers. When I ask what they mean by that, they usually say they lost a marriage. But losing a marriage doesn't make someone a loser in life! The truth is, we all win some things and lose others.

Being unsuccessful doesn't indicate you are a failure. If you fail second-grade math, you are not a math failure for life! Failing at something can be a growing, stretching experience if you're willing to put aside your emotions and learn from it. The fact that one marriage in your life has failed doesn't mean the second one will also fail. The key is to learn from your past mistakes.

Fear of Rejection

Few of us ever learn how to handle rejection. Many single-again people tell me they became single because their mate preferred someone else. Rejection can infuse you with poor self-esteem and guilt. These feelings can prevent you from attempting to build new relationships for fear of more rejection.

I'm told that some animals have an inborn sense of who will relate to them in a loving way, and who will kick them out of their path. As humans, we may be a little behind, but I suspect we're catching up. Our antennae receive the signals others send out, and the caution bells ring in our minds. If a rejection is in the wind, we run to safety.

Rejection often starts when we are young. When I was about six, I would head for the ball field, glove in hand, ready for a good game of baseball. At that age, I was almost always the smallest of the guys. When they chose teams, they usually tried to ignore me or put me so far out in the field that I couldn't even see home plate. The worst was that when it came time to bat, they tried to skip over me because I didn't hit well. After about seven innings, I usually felt pretty left out and rejected.

Over the years, I've learned that no one is universally accepted. No one has that much charisma or charm, but many have learned how to handle rejection. One of the best ways to handle rejection is by building your own self-esteem, inner confidence, and belief in your abilities. If you feel good about yourself, you won't be blown away by how others feel about you. If you are insecure, however, you will expect rejection, and then probably receive it.

Having people who deeply believe in us and our abilities helps us cope when we're shunned. We all question how good we are until someone else affirms us. Their love and affirmation can get us through some rough times.

Rejection can be a vehicle for learning. We can ask ourselves, "Why am I being excluded? Can I improve on these things in my life?" For example, if people stay away from me because I'm too reserved, I can find a way to conquer my shyness. If I'm too loud and brassy, and people stay at arm's length, I can learn how to be more gentle and personable. We can all gain from rejection!

The most important way to deal with rejection is to become secure in the knowledge that God will never turn His back on us. Throughout the Scriptures, God describes His love for and acceptance of us. He has promised never to leave us nor forsake us. We can be secure in the knowledge that we belong in God's family.

I'll have to admit that some of the members of God's family aren't always as accepting as God is. Not everyone views us the way God does. God's love for us isn't limited by our performance. His love is based on unconditional acceptance. When God loves us and we know it, we don't need to fear rejection. God's great promise of love to us is found in John 15:9, "As the Father loved Me, I also have loved you; abide in My love."

Fear of Marrying Again

Although many formerly married people would like to remarry, many who've gone through a devastating divorce fear it.

The biggest fear of remarriage seems to be that it won't work out and they'll have to endure another divorce. Many people want a guarantee. I wish I could give one, but there aren't any. The wisest counsel I can give is to make sure you have recovered from your divorce, and that your life is healthy and growing again. Too many people instantly remarry, trying to avoid the emotional whiplash caused by divorce. The pain and hurt are sidestepped, and all energy is directed toward the new relationship. The problem is that unfinished emotional work has a way of catching up with you down the road.

Time and building trust in a new relationship will remove some of the fears that accompany thoughts of remarriage. Premarital testing and counseling is another way to dismiss that fear. Reading one of the many books that deal with remarriage will also help. (See the reading list at the end of the book.)

Fear of marrying again, like the fear of putting your hand on a hot stove, is a legitimate one and deserves careful consideration.

Fear of Not Marrying Again

This fear is tied to the knowledge that you may remain single for the rest of your earthly life. It can mean dealing with acute loneliness and the fact that there may not be a "special someone" to take care of you in your later years when life and its infirmities catch up with you. Many single-again people list this as their number-one concern. Perhaps this explains the anxiety I often sense at some singles gatherings.

For many people, this apprehension can easily become the "great singles panic." It's somewhat akin to a condition back in my college days that we called the "senior panic." If a girl wasn't engaged by April of her senior year, she went into a state of panic. Everyone seemed to fear that all the men would disappear after graduation, and all the unmarried girls would be left alone forever.

In an attempt to curb this fear, many resort to placing ads in singles newspapers. Still others spend their money on computer programs that match up men and women. Singles cruises and holiday trips are other ways that people deal with this fear.

No one operates well in a state of panic or fear. My observation is that those who are the most relaxed, who seem to worry about it the least, are the first to remarry. People in a panic draw a lot of attention. So does a fire. A word to the wise would be: slow down long enough to let the right person catch up with you!

Fear of Being Hurt

Most of us deeply fear physical pain. When we were little and were taken to the dentist for the first time, we wanted to know just one thing—would it hurt? Many of us were lied to back then, and as a result, we are still trying to escape our dentist apppointments. He may be the most feared man in your town or your life. You just know that when you go there, you seldom escape without feeling some pain.

Pain is something most of us spend a great deal of time and money avoiding. We want to run when told, "No pain, no gain." The Scriptures tell us that suffering and the testing of our faith bring perseverance. Pain and hurt are necessary ingredients for all of us to grow.

How do you respond to hurt? Do you harbor it or let it help you grow? To be alive is to risk being hurt. It happens many times a day and in many different ways.

Writing for John Fischer's musical *The New Covenant*, composer Dale Annis's lyrics graphically portray what pain means:

We all get hurt.
We always seem to end up face-down in the dirt.
And hounded by the pain, we just remain
Satisfied to be hurt again.

We close our minds
To the meaning in the madness that we find.
We prefer to hide out, rarely try to find out
Just what pain is all about.

But if there's one thing you need to know,
It's that hurtin' only makes you grow.
And the pain you feel
Is the first step in being healed.

Yes, there's one thing you need to do,
It's to get your eyes off you.
Place them on the Lord,
And He'll make pain an open door.[1]

In this honest and touching song, we are told the truth about hurt. We all get hurt, but hurting helps to make us grow. Our pain is used for healing. God intends it to be an open door to our lives.

If all our pain were physical, we would know how to more effectively deal with it. But much of the pain we carry through life is emotional, and emotional pain usually subsides more slowly than physical pain. The hurt is inside your head and heart, and it's usually inflicted by other people. This kind of hurt can stay around for a long time. Often, the only path to healing is through forgiveness.

The Bible tells us that we are to practice unlimited forgiveness. Our example for this, of course, is Christ's simple request on the cross, "Father, forgive them; for they know not what they do" (Luke 23:34). Letting go of our hurts by forgiving others puts us on the road to healing. It also shows us how to deal with the pain that is yet to come. Life is a series of hurts and healings. The scars we acquire are simply badges of growth on the road to maturity.

Fear of Financial Needs

Where will the money come from to pay the rent or buy next week's groceries? What about the doctor bills and the car repairs? Few of us live beyond the concern of paying all of our monthly bills on time. Financial needs are a significant part of life for the single-again person. Many describe being single as the world of having "too little of everything that involves money."

Divorce can bring financial chaos to once stable families. The death of a mate without adequate insurance benefits can put enormous financial pressure on a family. The struggle to make ends meet with one wage earner is, at best, precarious. In the tough economic climate of the '90s, all of us may be moving rapidly from the age of more to times of less. How does the suddenly single person conquer this fear?

First, memorize and claim Philippians 4:19. There Paul affirms, "And my God will supply every need of yours according to His riches in glory in Christ Jesus." Notice that this verse talks about needs, not wants. God guarantees that our needs will be met.

Second, talk with your lawyer about your finances. He or she can give you a lot of sound advice on what to do with your money and assests and can also assist you in making some long-range plans regarding your finances.

Third, if you need the help of an accountant to put your finances in order, ask your friends for a referral. Tax laws and structures demand more than a layman's knowledge!

Fourth, sign up for a class on finances. Some classes are basic and some are advanced. Most colleges, junior colleges, and evening schools offer practical and effective courses.

Fifth, read a few good books that deal with the subject. There's a wealth of information on the market. Buy the practical ones, not the scare-tactic books that predict financial ruin for the world.

Finally, learn how to plan and live by a budget. Knowing what you have coming and going through your checkbook can give you a real sense of relief and send some of your money fears packing.

Fear of What Others Will Think

In small-town America 50 years ago, everyone knew his or her neighbor. Common problems and joys were public knowledge. They made for a closer community and deeper friendships. Behavior was somewhat modified by wondering, "What will the neighbors think?"

This can either safeguard from unruly behavior, or deter people from reaching out for growth in uncharted areas. Even in the '90s, we are still caught between the two extremes. Much of today's behavior is based on what others will think. Trends, fashions, and fads all focus on being "up" on things so that others will affirm us.

I've observed singles tell each other which "in" places to go to. The message is: if you go to the wrong singles hangout, others may not approve of you.

By daring to be different and feeling secure, you'll be able to deal with what others think of you. Since you'll never be able to please everyone, you may as well stop trying!

Many people spend their entire lives trying to satisfy others. It starts with trying to please Mom and Dad and win their approval. Then, it carries through to brothers and sisters and the entire extended family. People-pleasing spills out of the family and into other relationships. We even carry it into marriage and recreate the whole cycle in our own families. Sometimes, out of desperation, we scream, "I've gotta be me!" Trying to win the approval of others is a frustrating, never-ending process.

Many single-again people have discovered they can break free from the burden of always trying to live up to others' expectations. They simply refuse to worry about others' opinions and concentrate on developing who they really are, and what they want to become.

God and Fear

How does God feel about the fears that bind us and inhibit our growth? In 2 Timothy 1:7, the writer says, "For God hath not given us the spirit of fear; but of power, and of love, and of a sound mind" (KJV). This verse offers a clear alternative to the many different fears that dominate our lives. It tells us that fear does not come from God. Most of the time, it originates when we doubt God's ability to do things. Fear captures us daily when we forget that God is in charge of this universe and all that is going on within it. God promises us three things to replace the fear in our lives.

First, God promises to give us the *power* to win the battle against our worries. In the Old and New Testaments, we witness awesome displays of God's power at work. Some acts were so compelling that people developed a fear of God. In the New Testament, Paul talks about resurrection power that brings life out of death. As we give our fears to God, He bestows new life upon us, plugging us into His Spirit, the source of fear-removing power!

The second thing God gives us is *love*. It's a key ingredient in His fear-disposal kit. In 1 John 4:18, we read the promise that "perfect love casts out fear." Perfect love is always centered in our love for Christ and His love for us. It was that kind of love which gave Christ the courage to conquer any fear He might have had of the cross. I recently talked with a single man who expressed his own fear of dying. I tried to share with him that Christ had removed even that fear for us by His own death. Death is merely a promotion from this life to eternity.

Just prior to His death, Jesus revealed to His disciples what the power of what love could do. He encouraged them to "love one another" (John 15:17). Christ knew that His love would bind them not only to Himself, but to each other. Many single-again people have discovered that bond of love as they share with singles support groups across the country.

The third thing God promises is a *sound mind*. Have you ever wondered at the end of a long, hard day if you were going crazy? Perhaps too many things were cluttering your mind, making you feel out of control. All of us have such experiences. We start reacting instead of acting. Our competitive world has a way of squeezing the life out of the best of us.

When we have a sound mind, we have the mind of Christ in us. Those with a sound mind ask many times a day, "What would Christ do and say in this setting or situation?" The Scriptures set forth the pattern of how Christ lived and kept His sanity while on earth. His ways were usually contrary to the accepted form of behavior. In the same way, the behavior of the Christian single person in today's world will go against the grain.

A sound mind also indicates a peaceful one. But how do you get quiet long enough to have a little peace in this world?

I remember climbing Mount Whitney in the Sierras a number of years ago. The scenery was outstanding. What impressed me the most, next to my sore feet, was the peace and quiet we felt as we rolled into our sleeping bags late at night. It is probably the quietest place I have ever been.

In His final meeting with the disciples before the Crucifixion, Jesus gave them a gift to carry into the turbulent days ahead. He said, "Peace I leave with you; My peace I give to you" (John 14:27). He gave the very quiet of His own soul to the disciples. Perhaps what they failed to realize was that peace is not transferred that easily. It must be practiced. Unfortunately, the disciples too quickly became preoccupied with the sights and sounds around them.

Are you spending a lot of time perfecting your fears? Do you resolve one, only to transfer another into its place? Are you letting other people aggravate your fears? If you are, let go of your anxiety. Give it to God and let it become His problem. Start moving your life ahead again. Remember, no fear is bigger than God's power to conquer it. Fear has its focus on circumstances; faith has its focus on God!

Assessing Personal Growth

1. Write down one of your biggest fears.
2. When was the last time you allowed one of your fears to dictate your behavior?
3. Give an example of how you conquered a fear.
4. How would you tap into God's love to displace your fears?
5. How do you feel the people in your supportive community can help you resolve your fears?
6. Express any fears you might have about another marriage.

Chapter
Nine

Filling the Potholes

*"Faith never falls apart at the approach of the boulders of life.
It is when the rocks are rolling that faith shows up the best."*
Malcolm Smith

arry's recent divorce dropped him into the world of single-again people. As we talked at the conclusion of a singles conference, I asked him how his life was going. We discussed how he was raising the two children who were placed in his custody. As our conversation ended, Barry said his life was going along pretty smoothly; his only problem was avoiding the potholes in the road of life.

Walking away from our encounter, I began to think about the potholes that litter the path of the suddenly single-again person. Trying to avoid those ditches would be like attempting to dodge raindrops in a thundershower. A better solution would be to fill some of them in.

Let's take a look at the most common potholes a single-again person encounters.

Yesterday's Voices and Memories

You're driving home from work. At a stoplight, you glance out the window and spot a tiny French restaurant. Suddenly you burst into tears. You had your 20th anniversary dinner there and your mind flips into reverse, flooding you with memories of that night and the beautiful pearl ring your husband gave you. The rest of your evening is a disaster as you cope with tears and sort through memories.

I often receive calls from people I've counseled or who have attended my workshops. They describe similar experiences and then ask, "Am I moving backward in my growth? Why did I fall apart? Why wasn't I able to handle this?"

Our minds are like file drawers full of memories. Sometimes the drawers open when we least expect them to and dump our memory files all over us. We remember and laugh, or we cry, scream, get mad, and go on. Sometimes we embrace the positive memories and forget the negative ones. Other times we use the bad memories to deter our growth or flood our minds with self-pity.

When someone has hurt or wronged us, it's easy to feel we should cancel out all the good memories we shared with that person. A healthy response is to keep the good memories in our mental attic to dust off and enjoy occasionally. Never let a few bad memories wipe away the many good ones. Some people try to do this, often frantically searching for new relationships and new memories.

A word about bad memories: Don't dwell on them. Bad memories can cloud your future and rain on your parade. Bad memories should be like yesterday's newspapers—read and then put away.

Every experience in life is a potential memory. Sometimes we tend to let the bad memories overwhelm the good. Rachel told me that she'd permanently taken care of all her negative memories. She went through the family album with a pair of scissors and cut out her former spouse from every picture. Rachel's feeling was, "Out of sight, out of mind." If dealing with our memories were that easy, we would all be in better shape.

Good or bad, memories are a permanent part of our hearts and minds. They compose part of who and what we are today. There's no surgery to remove them. We simply live with and learn from them.

Special Times, Special Places

When I was about seven years old, I built my first and only tree house in a large cherry tree on our farm. It was several hundred yards from my home and quite secluded. I used it a lot during my grade-school years. My tree house was a special retreat. It housed my dreams and soaked up my tears. Years later, I visited my childhood home and climbed up into that old tree. Cramming my six-foot-one-inch frame into that small place, I stayed long enough to affirm that this place had been important to me during a special time in my life.

We all have tree houses, special times and places in our past that enrich our lives, creating important memories.

Becoming single again doesn't mean that the significant times that were once part of your life must end. Many single people seem to think their present crisis will cast a shadow over their lives forever. They believe that no experience, no person can ever bring sunshine into their lives again.

We make things special by investing ourselves in them. Just as I had physically and mentally outgrown my old tree house and moved on to my adult life, many of us need to outgrow the past, (as special as it may have been), and build some new memories.

As a single, have you ever thought that where you are can be a special time and place for you? Or is your primary concern to escape into married territory? Being single can be rich and worthwhile! What you build today will be the foundation for tomorrow. Singleness is not a detour, but a part of your life journey. Walk it slowly.

You Are Responsible for Making New Memories

Someone said that the only thing that makes the good old days the good old days is a poor memory. When people get older, their focus seems to shift into reverse. They become consumed with the events of yesterday, reminiscing that anything good that ever happened has passed.

In the last few years of his life, my grandfather was absorbed with the past. He would repeatedly tell stories about World War I and his childhood in England. He never tired of reciting the same tales. As he became older and weaker, Grandfather pushed even further into yesterday.

In the Bible, Moses wrestled with memories. As soon as he had led the Israelites out of Egyptian bondage, they began complaining about the quality of their food. Their minds were filled with the leeks and garlic of Egypt. The manna they were eating day after day simply lacked excitement. They had forgotten the beatings and inhumane treatment the Egyptian slavemasters had forced upon them. The Israelites saw little in their future but a combination of dust and more manna. The Promised Land was too distant to embrace. How wonderful yesterday had been, how horrible today was!

From time to time, all of us fall into that trap. Single people are certainly no exception. Like the Israelites, they look for someone to deliver them. If that deliverer can't save them, making better memories today than they had yesterday, they become disillusioned.

Who is responsible for making new memories? You are! Not your singles group, not your singles leader, not your relatives and friends. You are! Those around you become contributors, but you can't hold them responsible. When was the last time you reached out to someone and issued an invitation to join you in building a new memory?

As I look out at the sea of faces on the first night of a divorce-recovery seminar, I know those people have an enormous collection of hurts and bad memories that are connected to their divorce experience. In six weeks, however, amazing changes occur as those same people begin building new and positive memories together. For that to happen, each person has to do some reaching out. That kind of experience is often a "memory turnaround" for singles.

Many single-again people who lose a mate through death cling to memories of their former spouse. Even after remarrying, the former attachments remain. Singles who've remarried someone like this have later shared about the difficulty of inhabiting someone else's memory file. People need the freedom to build new memories.

Memories can be a ball and chain or a rare treasure. How many new memories have you placed in your file in the past year?

Those Long, Empty Evenings

I once asked a group of newly single people, "What was the toughest time of your day?" The overwhelming response? "The evening." Many said that everything went smoothly until they had to come home at night to either an empty apartment, or a single-parent household with all of its waiting problems. Then, the reality of being alone struck them. Some admitted to avoiding their home until late at night. They didn't want to face those empty hours until bedtime.

A young businessman, Jeremy, illustrated the loneliness he felt at the end of the day by telling me how much he missed having that "special someone" to talk with. Jeremy said that two dogs and a parrot didn't bring him much companionship, communication, or understanding.

The transition from marriage to being single again will often mean there won't be someone at home, waiting to help you fill empty evenings. If you don't plan your nights the way you arrange your days, the emptiness can haunt you.

Think about creative ways to handle your evenings. A class at a local college once or twice a week will give you something to look forward to. Developing a new hobby or taking music lessons can also be enjoyable. Deciding to read an interesting book and listen to some good music will make an evening pass rapidly and restfully. Include other people in your plans to fill those lonely times.

The greatest struggle with emptiness comes in the first months of being newly single. You quickly realize that you relied on your spouse to make most of your evening plans. Now you're doing the programming for yourself. Your toughest task will be forcing yourself to get going and start doing.

A few single parents have described their struggle to find time for themselves in the evenings. One mother told me she had no time for anything but housework and child care. I asked her if those jobs were planned or just there. Her response was that they were always there and she could never get away from them.

Overloaded evenings can be as bad as empty evenings. Both are a part of being single again. Both demand a plan and a purpose. Both will defeat you unless you are in charge. Don't allow your evenings to be potholes between your days!

Weekends

Friday at 5:00, millions of people leave their jobs with *T.G.I.F.* on their minds. Thanking God it's Friday has become a national pastime for both marrieds and singles. The weekend becomes a time of reprieve and catch-up for all the undone chores and tasks of the week. For many single-again people, however, it can be the loneliest 60 hours of the week.

If you are a noncustodial parent, the weekend means picking up your children for the visitation ritual. For the custodial parent, it may mean doing all the things left unfinished during the week. For both single parents, weekends can accentuate loneliness, highlighting the fact that you lack that special someone. When it arrives, Monday morning seems a deliverance from the empty weekend.

Weekends are when most singles groups really move into gear. The trips, parties, and special events help a person through those often lonely hours.

Doing things with other singles will help rebuild your social life. If your weekends have been lonely, start looking for an active and growing singles group in your community. Don't just be a social spectator—get involved!

I have discovered that many single-again people haven't entertained in their homes since their spouse left. Inviting a group of singles in often unlocks the door to developing a new world of friends.

Don't allow yourself to sit at home with your memories! Be a doer! Theater parties, concerts, square dances, hayrides, and maybe even a date are ways to make your weekends exciting.

The first question I ask singles is whether they have a support group of other singles they do things with. Some do, but many don't. All of them tell me how difficult it is to attend an event alone when they're used to going to activities with their mates. Well, don't go alone! Call up a few other singles and fill your car. Have dinner together, go to the event, and share your evening.

Find a group you enjoy being with. Make sure they are movers, not squatters. Some singles groups are dead, dead, dead! Someone just forgot to have the funeral. Doing fun things with other singles during that 60-hour gap will quickly make your weekends a time to look forward to.

Holidays

If weekends are bad, holidays are even worse. My counseling load always escalates in December. Many singles suffer from deep bouts of depression. Some spend their hours calling hot lines in cities across America. Others plan cruises to escape the loneliness. Most just grit their teeth and grind through the holiday season.

Holidays are traditionally depicted as family times. Your mind may go back to the special days when you were a child. You find yourself wishing for those times to return. The first Christmas without your former spouse is the toughest one. It seems as if the whole experience of losing your mate is dramatically highlighted during the Christmas season. You feel guilty for not being able to have the other parent there for the sake of the children. Inadequate finances prevent you from celebrating the season the way you once did. All this can put you in a blue funk. You scream about the commercialism of the season, yet feel bad that you can't buy all the gifts you'd like to give.

Many single-again people tell me they won't survive the holiday season. They always do.

Sharing Christmas with other singles can be a rewarding experience. They won't take anyone's place, but they will provide a community of love during a very special time. Many singles have an open house on Christmas Day and invite others to drop by and share the season with them. Because holidays are people days, opening your heart and home can add a great measure of warmth to your day.

When you start thinking about being alone at Christmas, think about how Mary and Joseph must have felt as they looked for simple overnight accommodations. The rejection they experienced is identifiable with yours. Their loneliness and frustration are yours. In spite of that pain, however, the birth of the King took place.

Most of the other seasonal holidays are endurable. They will be filled with lonely moments only if you allow them to be. You can make the choice to get lost in the holiday pothole or fill it with people, joy, and celebration.

Birthdays and Anniversaries

Special days in your personal life are tough times to live through when you become single again. The days that once called for celebration now seem to signal mourning. A celebration by one person sounds ridiculous, so you plan to ignore the event. Don't! Special times are the landmarks by which we measure life. Special times are the hinges on life's door. We need them, and we should plan to celebrate them.

One newly single man, Eric, told me he made his first birthday after his divorce a giant celebration. He invited old friends and many new single friends. Eric realized that his life still went on, even after a hurtful divorce.

Often, newly single people want to know what to do about a former spouse's birthday. I usually respond by asking them what they want to do. Follow your feelings and don't worry about being right or wrong. If you want to send a birthday card to your former spouse, do it! You may not want to throw a party for that person though, unless you have a very unusual post-divorce relationship.

Anniversary celebrations are different from birthdays. An anniversary is a milestone at the end of a year of marriage. When you are no longer married, the milestones end. Don't send hate messages to your former spouse or sit around feeling bad, remembering all your other anniversaries. File them and find a new way to spend your day.

An anniversary is a two-person event. A marriage starts it; a divorce or a death ends it. Let the memories stand, but put them in the back of your mind and leave them there. You can't live at the crossroads of those memories. You must choose to move ahead.

Family Reunions

Staying close to your in-laws after the death of your spouse is usually no problem. You receive love, care, and support from them. You are family, and death seldom changes that. But maintaining a long-term relationship with your in-laws after a divorce can be more difficult. The tension of who's right and who's wrong often becomes a family game. Sometimes you feel as though the teams are choosing sides and you are caught in the middle. If you have children, even the grandparent relationship can become tense. If your ex-spouse remarries, you may find that your in-laws' allegiance switches to his or her new mate.

Some divorced people have told me their in-laws still invite them to all the family events. They attend, even if their ex-spouse is present with a new mate.

I think the important thing is to decide what kind of relationship you'd like to have with your in-laws, and then pursue that. By the same token, your parents are in-laws to your ex, and he or she has the right to have a relationship with them, even if you don't like it. Divorce causes many breakdowns in family/relative structures. Remarriage can also bring you into another structure that is far from loving and stable. These scenarios often occur after divorce; yet no one thinks about them until they happen.

Both death and divorce eventually cause family ties to shift. Being family to someone can be and should be more than just a blood or marriage tie, though. It need not end simply because you are single again.

The single-again life is filled with many potholes. You can choose to hit every one of them, or you can try to steer around or fill them, moving ahead with your life. There are no pat ways to cope with potholes. You must simply try things that have a possibility of working. You must ask those around you what kinds of answers they've found to work through the difficult places. Then you take risks that will help you live on the growing edge of your new single life.

Assessing Personal Growth

1. How well do you feel you're doing at filing yesterday's memories?
2. What's the toughest special event for you to deal with as a single-again person?
3. How did you handle your first Christmas alone? If it's still in the future, how do you see yourself handling it?
4. What particular potholes are you having trouble filling right now?
5. Describe your current relationship with your former in-laws.

New Career Beginnings

"Never be afraid to trust an unknown future to a known God."

N ewly divorced and 53 years old, Faith stopped by my office on her way home from the employment agency. Amid a sea of tears and a deeply crushed spirit, she told me of her two-hour ordeal trying to find a job. After Faith had answered many questions and filled out a pile of paperwork, the counselor informed her that she had no marketable skills and would probably have to go back to school to obtain some training for the job openings available.

In the past 20 years of working with newly single-again people, I've heard this story hundreds of times. The only variable is the age of the applicant. The response is usually the same. Reality is that the world is not waiting to hire women who are suddenly single again.

A vast number of women who've experienced divorce must find a way to survive economically in an already overloaded job market. Many of them have been out of the work force for 20 to 30 years. The fact that they worked in a library when they were 22 has little bearing on job economics in the '90s. Many women dust off a 20-year-old degree in sociology or English, only to find that today's more skilled graduates form a long line in front of them.

A number of people I've met have switched from the employment line to the welfare line. Their anguish at losing a mate is compounded by their despair at not finding meaningful employment. In the working world, starting over is no easy task. The few who have worked during their marriages are the least affected. They simply continue on. The others often end up with meaningless, mundane jobs, hoping to get a few dollars coming in. Still others are convinced they'll never find a decent job, and begin to pursue a mate who will support them so they won't have to work.

Becoming single again, at any age, means starting many areas of your life over. Few things stay as they once were. Some of those changes can be welcome adventures and a source of growth. One such area is your career.

Pushing On

Many people already have satisfying jobs when they find themselves suddenly single again. The job may be so satisfying that they try to hide in it during their period of loss. Their former eight-hour day becomes a 16-hour day with overtime on weekends, in an attempt to push the pain away. My feeling is that many men try to deal with their emotional upsets this way. Some women do the same thing.

Work can become an obsession. It can also seem to be the only part of your life that you have any control over. A lack of achievement in marriage and family life can mean a frantic rush to gain some measurable success in your job.

On the other hand, pushing on in your present work can be a good form of therapy. It can take your mind off some of the problems you can't instantly solve. Work can fill potentially empty time, giving you a sense of fulfillment and self-worth.

Changes

When many things are changing around you, some by choice and some by chance, you have the opportunity to reevaluate every area of your life. One of the positive things that comes with being single again is the opportunity to take a long look at your job or career and ask yourself, "Is this really what I want to do?" I will admit that this is a risky question for anyone, single or married.

Several years ago I asked myself that question. My answer brought some profound changes into my life that moved me from the security of a church ministry to a national traveling and speaking ministry. I also discovered that you when you make this kind of drastic change in your life, you will run into two types of people.

The first kind of person questions your change, telling you that they wouldn't have done it if they were in your shoes. They dredge up a long list of fears, finally telling you they simply can't understand how you could do that kind of thing. They are discouragers.

The second type of person tells you how excited they are for you, and affirm your decision in every way. They are encouragers. We all need lots encouragers in our lives. We could do without the discouragers.

Too many people, while reevaluating a career decision, go from person to person, "pooling the ignorance." They ask everyone's opinion and either do nothing or follow the last piece of advice they heard.

Sound and trusted counsel is always valuable, but a collection of opinions just confuses the issue. I have considered the following questions several times in my life when I was faced with change. Get a pencil and answer them for yourself. It could mean the beginning of some changes in your career.

1. Why are you doing what you are now doing? Sometimes when I travel, I use this question to get acquainted with the people who pick me up at the airport. I usually ask them first what they do vocationally. They respond readily to that. When I follow it with a "Why do you do that?" question, I may get a confused look. Some answer by saying, "I've always done that." Others tell me they were trained for that special job years ago. Still others say that their family has been doing that certain job for over 100 years.

I'm sure all of these responses are legitimate, but I'm not sure they're always valid. Many people today are leaving jobs and careers they were trained for and are starting over. Sometimes the challenge is gone, and the career becomes a death sentence. I meet many people who are extremely unhappy with their jobs. I wonder why they continue to do them. Fear of change? Fear of what others will think? Fear of failure? Fear of financial loss? Fear of success? Probably a little of each.

Some people get into jobs temporarily until something else comes along. When nothing does, they simply settle into a rut after a while. Then they wake up 10 years later feeling locked in, wondering how they got there in the first place. If you take a temporary job, don't let it become permanent. That job is merely a passageway, leading you to the next part of your journey.

2. Are you happy and fulfilled in what you do? We spend many hours of our life working. If our jobs are exciting, rewarding, and challenging, we will be fulfilled. If they are a dull and weary experience, we will be miserable! That unhappiness will carry over into every area of our lives, affecting our families, children, relationships, and our own physical and mental health.

Feeling satisfied with your job is being happy while you are doing it, and happy with the results. It's doing the job well and meeting new challenges. When the challenge goes out of a job, boredom sets in. Weekends and holidays become release and relief from the job. What about your job makes you happy? Take your pencil and continue the list.

3. Is your present job the best investment of your talents and abilities? Each of us brings a vast assortment of abilities to any task in life. Some tasks call forth a wide variety of our skills. Others require very little talent. Unused abilities get rusty and decayed. Only the skills we use will stay sharp and honed. When was the last time you listed all of your abilities and talents? Have you had your close friends confirm what you see in yourself, as well as what they see in you?

One of the best ways to identify your own gifts is to have others call them out of you. A little-league coach, watching a new player swing the bat with confidence and ease, sees in him the power to be a hitter. The coach imagines him on a major-league team down the road. His job is to bring that skill out of the player and affirm it.

Some people are locked into jobs and careers that either misuse or ignore their abilities. Your personal satisfaction and happiness is at stake if you are in a position that doesn't use your abilities to their fullest.

The world has a lot of people in the wrong places. The key is not to remain in the wrong area! You can move, change, and make steps toward where you want to be. Take your pencil out again and list your gifts, talents, and abilities. Are you using them in your present job or career?

4. What would you rather do right now than what you are doing? If I left a blank space right here, I think I know the first thing many of you would write: Retire! Go to Hawaii or the South Seas to live! Never work again!

I lived in Florida for a number of years, and I used to watch the endless migration of retirees who had finally accumulated enough time and money to get the gold watch, and retire to a neat mobile-home park in the sun. For the first few months, they bragged that this was the way to go! After the initial excitement wore off, though, they started looking around for something meaningful to do with their time. Few could find anything. Many started drinking more heavily to escape their boredom.

Some things appear to be what we want until we get them in our grasp. It's like the child who wants many new toys and gifts for Christmas but ends the day playing with the empty boxes they came in.

My asking you to identify what you'd rather be doing isn't intended to send you on a flight of fantasy. It's intended to help you look at other possibilities for your life. Some people have dropped lifelong careers, and turned satisfying hobbies into new jobs. If you get more satisfaction and fulfillment from your hobby than your career, perhaps you should think about this kind of change.

Martha is a good example of a single-again person who made a hobby-to-career change. Her hobby was refurbishing old houses that were rundown and unmarketable. She started buying little ramshackle places that no one wanted. In a few short months, however, with her deft decorating skills, the houses were transformed and sold, often on the first day of their listing.

Martha slowly moved along buying, renovating, and reselling until before long, her hobby employed many others who worked with her. She often had four or five houses under repair at the same time. Soon she was buying larger and more expensive homes, giving them the same treatment. When I last spoke to her, she'd built a whole empire in the real estate world and had hired a property manager to keep track of all her holdings. Martha made the giant leap from a fun hobby to a prosperous career!

I've had some single-again people tell me their job or career brings joy to their life, and they'd rather do that than anything else. That's usually a good test of whether you're being fulfilled in your present situation. Either you are satisfied, or you are making too much money to change to what you really want to do. Take a minute and list your "rathers." Are some of them feasible? What would it take to accomplish them? Do you find yourself getting excited at the possibilities?

5. What did you want to do when you were a child? Most parents ask their children what they want to be when they grow up. If they want to be in a prestigious profession, the parents then brag to everyone within earshot that their Johnny or Mary is going to be a doctor, lawyer, and so forth. Some children grow up with their pre-cast careers taking shape around them. To follow any other would be a grave disappointment to their parents and others.

Many little boys who won speech contests in school were told by their parents that they would be great preachers someday. Thirty years later, they found themselves in a career they were ill-equipped to handle in any area other than speech. Childhood is a time to dream great dreams of tomorrow. For some of us, though, those dreams become obstacles that prevent us from doing what we really want to do. For others, the dreams are forgotten, replaced by more realistic pursuits. I'm not so sure that the things we showed great interest in as children should have passed away as we matured.

Being single again can be a time to think through some of those dreams, and perhaps begin pursuing them. It wasn't until my father's death that my mother was able to follow her childhood wish of becoming a nurse. For a number of years prior to her death, she was able to do something she'd always wanted to do.

Many children abandon their dreams because they're told by ill-informed parents that they are too stupid, too small, too unathletic, too poor in math, and so on. Many newly divorced people have told me their spouses had convinced them that they couldn't do certain things, only to discover after the divorce that this was untrue. Many of us will never grow up. We will be changing, growing, trying, and thinking new things throughout life. Don't be afraid to include childhood dreams in your plans!

Starting Over

A certain segment of the newly single-again population moves ahead, making changes. These are people who are changing from one thing they've been doing to another they desire. What about the mother with three children and 14 years of homemaking to her credit? With the death or divorce of a mate, her economic situation changes rapidly. In many homes, the mother must seek employment. With few up-to-date skills, where does she go? What does she do? Most major colleges and universities across America have added women's departments to their programs. One such program in our area is called "Reentry Options for Women." It deals with bringing a nonworking woman into the work force. It's not an employment agency. It goes well beyond that! The program interviews, tests, and educates women for what is available. Call your local community college today for available reentry programs you can enroll in.

The job market of 20 years ago is vastly different from that of today. Many jobs that existed then are now obsolete. Even your college major may be out-of-date. But new jobs and career opportunities are created every day, and many need people to fill them.

The old myth that a woman must take a "servant" job or position is long gone. In the past 20 years, many women have obtained positions once dominated by men. The women's movement has contributed to these advancements in many vocational fields, including the corporate world and the field of politics.

Educational opportunities abound. Just take a look at the listing of evening adult-education classes. It's incredible! Training is available for every conceivable job or career. Classes are held at convenient hours. Many are free, while others charge reasonable fees.

Perhaps the greatest fear a woman feels, when looking into a new or even a first career, is that her choice will be wrong. Don't let that deter you! You have the freedom to test the waters and move on to another situation if you choose. You don't have to be stuck in one career just because you started with it. That kind of thinking will trap your growth.

Be wary of getting into a specific field of employment just because there are numerous openings or the field offers great security. Neither of these aspects will mean much to you if you're unhappy with what you are doing. You need to do your homework and make sure that you want to try a certain area. Don't let others talk you into something you don't really want.

To get started, drop by your local college or university. Check out what it has to offer. Take the testing program. Sign up for a course or two. Investigate all the opportunities. Let yourself get excited!

Waiting to Be Rescued

A little earlier in this chapter and also in chapter 4, I mentioned those people who look around for someone to support them so they can avoid facing difficulty. Waiting to be rescued from singleness is deadly. First, you'll never know if you have what it takes to be responsible for your own life. Second, your knight in shining armor may deliver you from employment, but bring far more hazardous problems into your life.

Many single-again people are willing to make a trade-off in this area. I'm never quite sure they understand what's at stake. I can't stress enough the feelings of confidence, worth, and accomplishment that come from developing a new career.

New Careers and Jobs for Men

Divorce usually means that non-working women have to find employment. But what about the changes for men? Many continue to do what they've always done. Others use their single-again time to evaluate where they are vocationally.

Some men choose to move to new areas of the country after a divorce or the death of a mate. They want to make new memories and new beginnings. (For men with children who must remain with a former spouse, however, this is usually not a good option.) Other men go back to school. A few decide to change to another field of work. Ed recently confided to me, "I've always been in the career my wife wanted me to be in. Now, for the first time, I'm going to do what I want to do. I'm going to manage a resort."

Both men and women have found themselves in occupations prescribed by others. When those others no longer have control, they feel free to attempt new things.

Too Old and Tired?

Frequently, I speak with single-again people who are in their 50s or 60s. When they hear me talking about new jobs and developing new interests, they sigh and tell me they're too old and too tired to attempt anything. I'm always amazed by that response. As I read the Bible, I find that God doesn't seem to care much about age. Retirement isn't even mentioned in the Scriptures! Moses was well into his 80s when he undertook his greatest leadership assignment.

In the 20th century, Colonel Sanders and Grandma Moses were also late bloomers. Their successes came well after age 65. Many older singles seem content to serve time. Their unhappiness and lethargy is largely due to their lack of motivation and belief in themselves. Age has nothing to do with growth. New opportunities come to open minds and open hearts.

New Road Ahead

If you are past the crisis of losing a mate by death or divorce, it's time to start ahead. The future is in your hands! Don't get locked in a holding pattern. Spend some time asking yourself hard questions about your vocational possibilities. Find some trusted resource people and let them help you. Start planning for yourself. Take some of the little steps that will get you going. Celebrate your progress! You're on a new road!

Assessing Personal Growth

1. Why are you working at your present job or career?
2. Where would you like to be and what would you like to be doing two years from now? Five years from now?
3. How do you feel about starting over in a new field or vocation?
4. Have you ever refused a job because you were afraid to fail? Describe what happened.
5. Write down some of your vocational goals for the next five years.

Chapter Eleven

Catch the Serendipity Spirit!

"Life is, after all, made up of a series of moments
strung along the thin thread we call our destiny or direction."

Susan Muto

One black night, the three Princes of Serendip were riding their camels across the desert on a journey. Suddenly, they heard a voice telling them to dismount, reach to the ground, and pick up what they found lying there. The voice informed them that when daylight came, they could inspect what they'd picked up. It also revealed that they'd be both happy and sad at their discoveries.

When the light dawned, they reached into their pockets and found they'd picked up precious gems. The princes were elated they had taken as many as they did, but disappointed that they hadn't taken more.

Catching the serendipity spirit in your life is making the same discovery those three princes did. Being single can be a serendipity experience for you! You have the chance to pick up many things that will enrich your life while you are single. They may not appear to be dazzling jewels to you right now, but down the road you might be surprised at what you possess.

In this chapter, I want to share some of the serendipities connected with singleness. To help you really appreciate those serendipities, first let's take a few minutes and look at attitudes toward single life.

1. Fearing singleness. Are you living in fear about being single? In an earlier chapter, I said that fear can immobilize a person. Many people are so afraid of all the things they've heard about singleness that they simply want to run away and hide from it. The things we fear most, however, seldom happen to us.

Tanya once told me that she'd tried to come to our singles group for three consecutive weeks, but her fear prevented her from getting out of the car once she was in the parking lot. For three weeks Tanya drove in, drove around, and drove out. On the fourth week, she parked but sat in her car, afraid to go in the door. But just as she was about to start up her car and drive out, a woman tapped on the window, inviting her to go into the meeting. To this day, she probably wouldn't have made it inside if a caring person hadn't noticed her anxiety. Tanya's final comment to me was, "I really enjoyed tonight. I don't understand what I was afraid of."

What are your greatest fears of singleness? You could be fighting a paper dragon.

2. Hurting in singleness. Are the hurts you acquired in your marriage carrying over into your single life? Some single-again people who have experienced a divorce spend all of their physical and mental energy trying to get even with their former spouse. They've been hurt, and now they want to hurt in return.

Other hurts come from the people around you who don't understand your situation. They judge, condemn, and indict you because they haven't been there, or taken the time to listen.

Another hurt comes from the guilt you place upon yourself. You absorb this inwardly, but the results are manifested outwardly. It's easy to spend a great deal of time licking wounds and buying bandages. Sometimes it takes more energy to remain hurt than to let yourself heal.

In divorce-recovery seminars, I watch as people let go of their pain by forgiving others. Anger and pain are replaced by smiles. Healing begins with the decision not to hug your hurts any longer.

Are you placing your pain at the top of your list? Are you looking for vengeance? Clutching your hurt will only rob you of recovery.

3. Adjusting to singleness. Adapting to new life situations is like buying a new pair of shoes. The old ones are always more comfortable, but they look less respectable. New shoes are stiff, squeaky and usually uncomfortable for a time. This changes once you've worn and broken them in. It's not an overnight experience.

New shoes and new people are a lot alike. Many people take each other for granted during marriage. You can't bring this attitude into the singles world, though.

Having to face what I sometimes call "second adolescence" makes single-again people feel as if they've been placed in a time capsule and shot back to their youth. The pressures of dating and relating to members of the opposite sex again can prompt you to scream "Foul." A sense of unfairness and a "Why me?" attitude can consume a lot of your mental energy if you are not on your guard.

Are you willing to adjust slowly to your new singleness? Are you willing to take time and trust the experience?

4. Accepting singleness. Accepting singleness usually starts in your head. You may have to admit that this isn't where you planned to be or even wanted to be at this time of your life. You may, in fact, detest being single. But accepting it is knowing that whatever you think or feel, being single is reality for now.

I counsel many single-again people to cultivate the habit of saying, when asked, that they are single *now!* That doesn't mean forever. It means for now. I meet some newly single people who seem to regard singleness as a permanent form of punishment.

You can face singleness only if you are willing. Some new singles try to hide out with married people. They feel secure with them and can pretend that they too are still married. That's not healthy. It's a game they will ultimately lose.

As you accept singleness, you'll find that world is populated with some of the nicest people you have ever met. Are you accepting or denying where you are?

5. Trying to escape singleness by marriage. When people lose a mate either by death or divorce, they often find themselves emotionally vulnerable. They become very susceptible to any form of attention from the opposite sex. It's easy to confuse caring with loving. I watch many single people marry someone who cared for them when they were hurting. A few months into the new marriage, though, they find they have very little in common. Often, a second divorce takes place within a year or two of that marriage. Many of these failed second marriages are simply emotional collisions.

Other singles try to remarry quickly in order to get even with their former spouses and prove they can catch someone. Still others are so afraid of being alone that they attach themselves to any warm body.

Are you looking for an easy exit from singleness? If you are, you'll probably find one. Look out! It may be a dead end.

6. Enjoying singleness. Every single-again person experiences an initial period of chaos and confusion. People arrive at singleness by different routes. Some who've lived in deteriorating marriages look upon singleness with relief. Others who were happy in wedlock look upon singleness with fear. It takes a year or two to put the past behind, and begin to build new memories. There will come a day down the road when you'll look around at where you have been. Then you'll examine where you are, and where you are headed, and stop just long enough to cheer. Part of your joy will be knowing how much you've grown. The other part will be anticipating what's ahead.

You let go of a tremendous load when you begin to feel good about where you are, knowing that you no longer have to look for a "quick out." I meet many single men and women who are enjoying every aspect of their singleness. As one meticulous man said, "When you come home to your apartment at night, you find everything just as you left it. If you can't find something, then *you* misplaced it."

Now that you've taken an honest look at your attitude, let's go on to the serendipities.

Freedom of Choice

In marriage, your freedom of choice is sometimes dramatically restricted by either the dominance or dependence of your mate. Your life can seem like a computer disk that's programmed and run each day by your spouse. You merely perform what's planned for you. Your choices can be limited, and your joys few. Becoming single again often sets a person free from stifling control. Initial freedom from that kind of bondage can make you feel uncertain. Programmed people are performers. Now they need to learn to initiate things for themselves.

The myriad choices single life offers can be very confusing. Sometimes there are too many options too soon. You wonder if you're making the right decisions or the wrong ones. Making choices for yourself is both liberating and frightening, but remember what I said earlier—you have the freedom to fail.

Take a few minutes and list the different choices you have as a single-again person. I'll suggest a few; you add yours.

I can eat any kind of food I like.
I can eat anytime I want.
I can live anywhere I choose.
I can work at anything I like.
(Keep going! I can . . .)

Don't look around to get approval before listing your choices. You give yourself permission!

Joyce told me she was going to become a mechanic after her divorce was final. She said she'd always wanted to tinker around with cars, but her husband told her it wasn't ladylike and she would get greasy and dirty. She no longer needed his consent!

You can live where you want and how you want. Maybe you lived with Mr. or Mrs. Clean all your life. Now you can leave the newspaper on the floor once in a while!

Julie approached me at the end of a workshop and invited me to come to the parking lot to see her new car. She was a quiet, reserved, gray-haired woman of about 45. I had a mental picture of a nice conservative Ford or Chevrolet four-door in a deep maroon color. We walked past three of those. Then she pointed to her car—a bright blue and white Mustang with racing stripes, air scoops, spoilers, mag wheels, sun roof, custom stereo, and a giant whip antenna! My shock made Julie smile, and she told me why she bought it. That's right, you guessed it: 20 years of driving the cars her husband chose. Nice, quiet, conservative cars. Finally, she had the freedom to choose something she'd always wanted. Second adolescence, you say? No way! Just a person who wanted to make her own decisions for a change.

The adventure of a new job is another choice often denied those within the structure of marriage. I've witnessed people literally coming alive with excitement as they make their own career choices. The options are limitless! Take the risk!

Someone poignantly described risk-taking like this:

To laugh is to risk appearing the fool.
To weep is to risk appearing sentimental.
To reach out for another is to risk involvement.
To expose feelings is to risk exposing your true self.
To place your ideas, your dreams, before the crowd is to risk their loss.
To love is to risk not being loved in return.
To live is to risk dying.
To hope is to risk despair.
To try is to risk failure.
But risks must be taken, because the greatest hazard in life is to
    risk nothing.
The person who risks nothing, does nothing, has nothing and is nothing.
He may avoid suffering and sorrow.

But he simply cannot learn, feel, change, grow, love and live.
Chained by his certitudes, he is a slave.
He has forfeited freedom.
Only a person who risks is free!

You Don't Have to Ask Permission

I remember how embarrassed I used to get in elementary school when I had to raise my hand and get permission to go to the washroom. Many times, I wished that I could just sneak out and back. Most of us learned back then that life is an endless series of having to ask permission. You simply can't live and do your own thing at others' expense.

There is, however, a fine line between structure and enslavement. Many formerly married singles still feel they must ask their former spouses' permission to do certain things. They say they have a hard time with their new freedom. Others admit that, initially, they didn't mind asking their spouses for approval before doing certain things. What bothered them was that soon their mates imposed heavy restrictions, limiting their freedom. Many were belittled for so long that they simply became subservient to their spouses.

Being single again means that you can give yourself permission to do something. You don't have to ask others if it's all right. Those choices I just talked about are really yours!

There's a poem titled "Ambivalence" that I often share with people in my workshops. One of the key lines says,

"I give myself permission to change in the way I think best
and not box myself in with the expectations of others,
to learn to be my own person and not forever live in the past."

You have permission—yours! What changes do you need to make in your life?

You're Not Owned by Anyone

The bridegroom, Kevin, walked around greeting guests at his wedding reception. As he talked with another couple, I overheard him say, "Well, she's mine now!" As Kevin said it, he hugged his wife to his side. At that moment, his wife probably felt good about the comment and didn't give it a second thought. Ten years later, though, that same comment could become a noose around her neck.

Marriage is not ownership. There is a world of difference between being owned and belonging. Many men and women have the idea that marriage creates ownership.

There are three kinds of relationships in marriage. *Dependence* is the kind of relationship where one person leans on and counts on the other person to meet all of his or her needs. *Independence* is a relationship where each person operates on their own, and works with their spouse only when necessary. *Interdependence* is a shared relationship, with two people participating in all the things that a marriage can be.

Many marriages that end in divorce were ownership relationships; one mate felt the other was his or her personal property. This type of marriage can cause the newly single person to be dependent, or it can create disdain for getting close to anyone again. Many singles live reacting to former ownership, loudly telling everyone they are their own person. This response usually just drives people away.

Being your own person means you want to be allowed the space to reach out and grow. You have a good, sound mind that can make choices and decisions. Your life, in or out of marriage, is always a *shared* existence. If anyone has to own you, let it be God. The great thing about having God in your life is that He lets you make choices. He simply promises to be your Friend and give you guidance.

Set Your Own Priorities

I sat down the other day and made a long list of things to do in the upcoming week. As the list got longer, I started to panic, wondering how I'd get everything done. I began worrying, and then my brain turned numb. As the lines and items on the paper started swirling, I shoved the list aside, resolving to do something fun, an activity that would deliver me from having to confront my list of realities.

Wisdom would have been to go over the list and put a 1 beside all the things that are top priority, a 2 next to others, and a 3 or 4 beside the rest. And instead of getting discouraged and avoiding my work, I should have followed the words on a little inspirational sign: *The difficult we do right away; the impossible takes a little longer!*

Learning to sort out your priorities is a lifetime process that demands constant attention and reevaluation. Many times, your priorities will collide with the preferences of others. Anyone in leadership, for example, knows how difficult it is to sell your list to those who work under you. What's important to you invariably will be in second or third place to them.

Even more, priorities constantly change. The spotlessly clean house you once took pride in somehow seems less important now. Old rules and regulations may seem rather insignificant now that your situation is different.

There is a growing list of services designed to aid busy people. I recently read of a service that will come to your home and help organize your closet and wardrobe. That sounds exciting to me; yet, my fear is that I'll end up being programmed by someone else. Some days I would welcome that; other days, never!

I am responsible for my life, and I must set my own priorities with God's help and direction. Many single people I meet struggle in this area. Their priorities get jumbled by the people passing in and out of their lives.

What are your priorities? Can you spend a few minutes right now and make a list? Rate them in order of importance. After you've worked on your list for a while, evaluate how much time you are giving to those priorities. It might even be a good idea to record the priorities you had before you became single again, and compare it to your list now. Once you've done this, understand that prioritizing is not a once-and-for-all experience. Revising, updating, and reorienting are an ongoing process.

How many of your priorities are dictated by someone else? Taking charge of your life again means that some of those priorities must be your own. Here are some common priorities that newly single people often give.

1. Personal time. You need time to do the things you enjoy. Read, sleep, rake leaves, ride a merry-go-round, walk in the rain, read poetry, window shop, see a friend.

2. Children. Many newly single people are also newly single parents. Raising children with both parents in the home is difficult enough. Doing it by yourself is even more challenging. Your children need quality time with you, and you need quality time with them.

3. Job. Does work dictate your entire life? Are you able to keep it in perspective with your other responsibilities? Do you take it home with you in the evening and on weekends? Is it causing you more misery than happiness?

4. Social life. Do you have any leftover time and energy to spend socially with other singles? Do you set apart time on your weekly calendar for this outlet? Are you building a new circle of single friends? Sometimes when we get overloaded with our long lists of things to do, a good question to ask is, "Will this really matter 100 years from now?" If you want to be more realistic, will it even matter next month? Becoming suddenly single again means that you are responsible to set your priorities. Don't let meaningless tasks dictate your life and eliminate your fun!

5. Church life. Being a Christian is vital to your life. Being a part of a church, a community of faith and love, is also essential for growth. Find a place where you can grow spiritually and serve God joyfully.

How to Experience a Serendipity

We've all gone to various events in our lives that we predicted would be dull, boring, uneventful, and a waste of time. Sometimes, one of these functions becomes a serendipity. We expect one thing and are quite surprised by another. We go away acknowledging how happy we were to have attended.

Look for the small serendipities in life. Maybe the party you went to didn't live up to your expectations, but someone you met there made the evening shine. Sometimes a simple, affirming conversation with another person becomes a special event. Serendipities are sprinkled throughout life. Most of us spend so much time looking for the big ones, we miss all the little surprises. Expect them to happen to you and they will. When they do happen, celebrate!

Learn to be a giver of serendipities. You can make someone's day by sending him or her a card of encouragement, giving a warm hug, or picking up the phone and calling a faraway friend. To receive serendipities, you must also give them. Someone once said that love isn't love at all until you give it away. You are in a special place in your life. Catch the Serendipity Spirit!

Assessing Personal Growth

1. Of the five attitudes toward singleness described in this chapter, which one do you most identify with?
2. Do you still look for someone to give you permission to try new things?
3. Name your top three priorities right now.
4. Describe a serendipity that happened to you recently.
5. Describe a serendipity you were able to give to someone else in the past year.

Chapter Twelve

New Pathways: Remarriage

"It is far more difficult to create a second marriage than a first,
when children are involved . . . and it is more important to succeed.
The stakes are higher. The risks are greater.
And everybody involved knows it."

Judith Wallerstein

Tim and Holly smiled warmly at me as I pronounced them man and wife. They embraced and then moved slowly to the unity candle. They looked at each other lovingly as they lifted their candles to the unlit candle. When it caught the flame, they blew out their candles and returned them to the stand. As they moved back toward me, I invited their children to join them for prayer at the altar as we concluded the ceremony:

Lord, we thank You for the vows of marriage shared at this altar today. Now, as these children join hands in a circle of prayer with their parents, we ask Your blessing upon the blending of these two families into one unit.

Lord, we know this union will perhaps be the most difficult of all. It will take time, great portions of patience, generous amounts of love, and the wisdom of gentle discipline. With Your help and guidance, together we can make it.

Lord, guide this new family unit as they share the joys and struggles of life in this adventure in love. Amen.

This remarriage ceremony wasn't just a union of two people, it was a joining together of two families. Tim had three children by a former marriage; Holly had two children. Now, they both had five and would be living in the same house after the honeymoon.

After the wedding, my mind drifted back to the time when both of these single-again people joined one of my divorce-recovery classes. They were coming out of ugly and demeaning divorces. Any thought of ever remarrying was not part of their agenda. They both felt bitterness, hurt, anger, and guilt. But now, almost two years later, they were starting a new life together.

Seeing people remarry is one of the rewards of working with wounded lives. Watching singles move through the devastation of divorce into a new life filled with hope and optimism is a big victory.

But remarriage is not without its struggles.

Before you run out, order your wedding invitations, and book the local chapel, let's go back and examine the pathway that leads to the remarriage altar.

Let's stop here at the beginning and admit that the Bible does speak to the issue of remarriage. Matthew 19 and 1 Corinthians 7 have verses that, frankly, are not very poplular in the modern setting. And they are often interpreted in various ways. In fact, I've collected a fairly fat file of various white papers, articles, and even books on the subject, many of which disagree sharply with each other.

The Bible seems to speak most directly to individuals who *initiate* a divorce—many of whom, unfortunately, no longer care what God or the Bible says. If, on the other hand, you're someone who had divorce forced upon you, the picture is cloudier.

Rather than lay down a firm theology here, I would really encourage you to talk with your own spiritual leaders. Find out what your church believes and why. Sort out this difficult question under the guidance of those God has placed in leadership over you, so that you can proceed with a clear conscience.

(For the position held by the publisher of this book, Focus on the Family, see Apendix B.)

The Reality of Remarriage

I believe that 90 percent of all the single-again people I meet would marry again if they could find the right person. Women frequently ask me, "Where are all the men my age?" Men also question, "Where are all the good women hiding?" Both seem to pass each other without noticing, and continue their search.

The opportunity for remarriage for people in their 20s and 30s is much greater than for those in their 40s, 50s, and 60s. A quick visit to the three largest singles groups in your city will quickly reveal the uneven ratio of women to men. In most cases, you'll find a large membership of women over 40 and a small group of men the same age.

There are several reasons for the imbalance. First, men tend to be more vocational and recreational in their interests and lifestyles; women who aren't employed tend more toward the relational. Men are usually more guarded in sharing their feelings and struggles; women are usually more open and comfortable with expressing themselves. Men usually initiate new relationships while women often stand around, waiting to be asked. Men are taught to be resourceful and to solve their own problems; women talk with other women to seek help with their frustrations. A man will resist going to a counselor, fearing he will be unmasked, and his male ego endangered. A woman more readily turns to counseling and is often more open and receptive to help.

I've watched men walk into a singles meeting, do a quick tally of the number of women versus men, and make a speedy exit. No man in his right mind wants to join a women's group! He'd rather be on the golf course, or working alone in his garage on a hobby.

Another reality in the world of remarriage is that middle-aged men tend to date women 10 to 12 years younger. A group of women from our 40s class came to me one Sunday morning and asked permission to raid the 30s class. They wanted to get back all the 40-year old men. We laughed about it, but the sting of truth was there. It may not be fair, but it happens. I've asked some men how they feel about this. A few admit that dating younger women makes them feel good. It bolsters their ego and helps them feel young. It sort of says, "Look what I have!"

From an older woman's standpoint, this attitude can become a reminder that aging seems to work against women and for men.

What happens when an older man marries a younger woman? I'll never forget a counseling session I had with a couple a number of years ago. It was one of those "May-December" unions, and it didn't appear to be working out. I remember hearing strong comments from the woman as I gently explored the problem. It seemed to her that everything she wanted to buy or do brought one comment from her new husband, "I've already done that!" He had little interest in the things she wanted to explore in life because he'd lived longer and experienced all those things before. He simply wanted to settle down, periodically take his young wife out for public viewing, and then go home and watch television by the fireplace. This situation highlights one of the grave dangers of "spring-winter" relationships. One person is an explorer, the other is a settler. The tension this kind of relationship produces can cause a speedy second divorce.

Steve had been single for 12 years. He was handsome, articulate, and a successful businessman. When I asked him jokingly why he hadn't latched onto one of the sweet young ladies in the singles group, he looked at me intently and said he was looking for a relationship, but wanted one with someone his own age. He explained that he wanted someone who was on his level experientially. He added that he was looking for maturity in a woman, not just youthful attractiveness. Several years later he married a woman one year younger than himself. They are still married today!

Cautions on the Pathway to Remarriage

Pamela approached me at the coffee break during a singles seminar asking, "How long should a person wait after a divorce is final before dating again?" I wish I could give a list of recommended times for different situations, but I don't have enough paper for that. However, I can suggest some guidelines that apply to every single-again person.

1. Don't start dating until you are emotionally ready for a new relationship. You can actually fall for a person on the first date. Your heartstrings may give the go signal, but your emotions might have you on hold.

2. Don't begin dating until you have stopped talking about your former spouse and telling all your "divorce war stories." No one wants to spend an evening being bombarded with stories of how bad and terrible it was (and is). If you're still talking and thinking divorce, stay home.

3. Don't date just to prove to yourself and your former spouse that you can get a date. If you are a woman and your former spouse has run off with a pretty young secretary, you may find yourself wanting to prove something.

I remember the woman who told me her way to get back at her husband was to sleep with as many men as she could. She had been faithful all during her marriage; but when she found out he was having an affair, she decided to get even. For two years after the divorce, she jumped from bed to bed. She finally woke up and realized she was playing a losing game. She didn't need to prove anything.

4. Don't date just to relieve your loneliness. You may fill an evening, but you won't solve the problem.

5. Don't be afraid to share emotional honesty with your date. Be yourself; enjoy the experience and the company of other people. Remember, no one is "so cool" that they don't falter and sputter in a few places. Feel free to laugh at yourself.

6. Don't take your memory file along when you go on a date. Sitting in a restaurant and telling your date that you and your former spouse spent meaningful moments there will not get you high ratings.

7. Dating after many years of marriage may make you feel like an adolescent again. Accept it and don't worry about it. Adolescents don't fret too much about tomorrow; they enjoy today. Try to do the same.

8. (I may get into trouble here!) If you are a woman, I believe it's all right to ask a man out once in a while. I believe that men like to be asked every so often instead of always taking the initiative. And if you experience rejection, you'll know how the last man you rejected felt.

Taking Your Time

Many people want a quick return on the investment of their time with another person. Some want to be paid with sexual involvement; others want to be paid with a marriage ceremony.

I can recall many phone conversations over the years that started like this:

"Jim, this is Bill. Are you free on Saturday, the tenth of June, at three in the afternoon?"

"Yes, Bill, I'm free. What do you have in mind?"

"Jean and I want to get married, and we'd like you to perform the ceremony."

"I didn't know you two were that serious!"

"Well, it's not the quantity of time, it's the quality."

"How long have you been going together?"

"Two months, but we're really in love!"

Does that sound familiar to you? When I ask people like Bill and Jean to take their time, they get offended and usually call someone else who can use $50 for a quick tying of the marriage knot. Hurrying a new relationship to the altar can short-circuit it, leaving you to wonder what happened.

Over the past 20 years, I have seen many second marriages end in divorce because the people involved didn't give the relationship time to mature. My rule of thumb is that a new relationship takes from 12 to 18 months before it's ready for the altar. I applaud the people who take their time. There is much more to a second marriage than setting the date and walking down the aisle.

Getting to know your new love's children takes a while. A second marriage doesn't create instant family; it just puts everyone under the same roof. Becoming a family takes time before the wedding and even more time after the ceremony. Instant adjustments seldom happen.

One friend of mine kept her new romance under wraps. When it was time to set the wedding date, she brought her new man home and simply announced to her three children that he would be their new daddy. They all stood looking at him with their mouths open. They had met him only once, briefly, and now he was coming into their lives forever. Their negative reaction and stiff resistance kept the relationship on ice for a number of months.

It takes time and many shared experiences to feel love for another person's children. The children need as much, if not more, time to feel comfortable with you.

I've seen unhappy children ruin second marriages. I've watched them pit parent against stepparent in a contest that no one wins. If you are building a new relationship with another person, take the time to share love with his or her children.

Getting to know and love extended family takes as much time as it does to warm up to the children. Remarriage means inheriting instant in-laws and relatives. Some will approve of your new union, others will not. You may find yourself locked in the struggle of trying to win their approval. Try to let those new relationships grow gradually. It's difficult to crash into the middle of someone's life and receive instant acceptance from his or her relatives. Spend time with all of them before you get married. Let them know you as you really are. Love and acceptance can never be forced.

Why Second Marriages Fail

After 20 years of watching people divorce and remarry, let me draw some observations as to why second marriages fail. You might use these reasons as a preventive guideline when building new relationships.

1. One person isn't ready for remarriage.
2. One pushes the other into remarriage.
3. One attempts to "save" the other, causing an emotional collision.
4. One or both drag emotional baggage from the former marriage into the new relationship.

5. One or both are unwilling to invest what it takes to produce growth.
6. One or both don't take enough time to get to know each other's families.
7. Neither person shares his or her dreams with the other.
8. Neither person shares his or her history with the other.
9. Relational growth gets short-circuited by a quick remarriage.
10. One person refuses outside help when it is needed.

This is a short list. You might add your own potential danger signals. Remember, once emotions take over in a relationship, rational thinking vanishes!

Rejoining the Married Community

In a premarital counseling session I was conducting, the woman began to cry. When I asked what the problem was, she told me how sad she felt to leave her singles group and move back into the married group. She added that the singles had become her family after her divorce and had walked with her through many battles and struggles over the past three years. Now she was changing communities again, and she wondered how she would be received as a "remarried" in the world of the "still marrieds."

Several years ago, three remarried couples came to me in a church I was serving and asked to start their own Sunday education class. They had tried several married classes but felt they just didn't fit in. Since they had special needs and struggles, they wanted their own group. We started a new class for them and called it the "Illuminators." Within a year's time, the class had over 30 couples, all of whom had remarried. This is one creative way to handle the problem of reentering the married world.

Some remarrieds have said they were made to feel like second-class citizens when they attempted to move back into the married community. Few people tried to understand what they'd gone through or even what they still had to go through as remarrieds. Sometimes, it helps to patiently share your journey with others who haven't been there. At other times, you simply have to find the people who've been where you are, and begin rebuilding with their help.

One woman told me recently that her biggest problem in remarriage was meeting other marrieds who seemed to enjoy reminding her that she'd been married before.

The people around you won't always be understanding. Some can be downright cruel. Eventually, though, you'll learn to smile at time-worn comments and jabs directed at you, and continue to build your life.

A New Pathway

Remarriage is vastly different from a first marriage. It's more complicated and demanding in every area. It takes hard work to make it happen. More second marriages fail than first marriages. Although many people will choose remarriage and make it work, others will find themselves in a second divorce.

Making a second marriage work requires asking God for His help. He's in the rehabilitation business; He helps people start over again. God gives a person the strength and wisdom to make a second marriage grow.

There are many bumps in the road to remarriage. Take your time to navigate them carefully. Ask your friends for help, and trust God to give you a new beginning for your life.

Assessing Personal Growth

1. How do you feel about a woman asking a man out?
2. How long do you feel you should know a person before you consider remarriage?
3. What still has to happen in your life before you will be ready for remarriage?
4. What are your greatest fears about remarriage?
5. How do you think God feels about remarriage?
6. How does the thought of never remarrying make you feel?

Chapter
Thirteen

Learning to Wait

"He who hurries delays the things of God."

St. Vincent de Paul

I hate to stand in line! It feels like a giant waste of my time, and I don't know what to do while I'm waiting. I go to great lengths to avoid lines. When traffic moves too slowly on our California freeways, I try to dodge the congestion on side streets. Even if it takes longer, I'll do it to avoid sitting in traffic. I leave ball games early so I won't get caught in the lines of cars waiting to exit the parking lot. I'm definitely not a good "wait-er." But I'm a lot better than I used to be.

The Army is often referred to as the place you "hurry up and wait." Life is a little like the Army. You and I rush here and there, but we still find ourselves doing a lot of waiting. Impatience seems to increase with age. We don't want to hurry through the end of our life journey, but we don't like standing around, waiting for the finish line either. Perhaps the secret of a well-balanced life is to know when to run and when to rest.

Our basic problem with waiting is wondering if life is passing us by while we're on hold. I've heard there are three kinds of people in life: those who make things happen, those who watch things happen, and those who don't know what's happening. Perhaps we can add a fourth: those who never learn to wait so that the right things will happen.

Solomon tells us there is a time for everything. He ends his long list with a word of promise in Eccl. 3:11, "He has made everything beautiful in its time."

There's a vast difference between waiting in limbo and living in it. Limboland is populated by people who can't use waiting creatively. They simply plop on the curb, sitting motionless until someone presents them with a game plan. If it fits their lifestyle, they adopt it and move on. If not, they reject the plan and wait for a better one. They are often pessimists who blame their present state on past experiences. They carry signs saying, *"Help! Someone rescue me from waiting!"*

In my 20 years of ministering to single-again men and women, I've discovered two kinds of "wait-ers"—those who creatively wait, plan, and move their lives ahead, and those who look for someone else to do it for them. Let me suggest some areas in which you need to practice and perfect how to wait.

First, you need to wait for and wait before the Lord. If you've made a decision to live for God, you will soon learn that you can't live ahead of Him. Since God has the plans for your life in His hand, you'll have to wait each day until He reveals them. The easiest way to begin this practice is to quietly present yourself to the Lord at the beginning of each day and say, "Here I am, Lord. I'm waiting for Your direction and instructions." As a friend of mine says, "Then be quiet long enough to hear what God is trying to say back to you." It's easier for most of us to spend our time dictating letters to God than receiving His words to us.

Isaiah tells us the benefits that waiting before the Lord can bring. In Isaiah 40:31 he says, "But those who wait on the Lord shall renew their strength; they shall mount up with wings like eagles, they shall run and not be weary, they shall walk and not faint." Most of us forget the waiting; we just take off and start running!

Many people who've been single for a number of years after a divorce feel that waiting is all they do. They wait for circumstances to change, for their career to take off or crash, for a special someone to come into their life, for the seasons of life to come and go; they wait to make more money so they can pay more money for things that keep costing more money. They wait for a serendipity that will rescue them from waiting. And they keep waiting on and on.

I believe the tension and burden of waiting will ease up when people concentrate on waiting upon the Lord. When you start there, it puts all the stress and frustration in the Lord's hands. It doesn't mean you give up; it means that you give in and put waiting in the right perspective. It's exciting to wait for the Lord to guide: He will give you perfect directions!

For the moment, I'm waiting to see when I can finish writing this book. While I'm waiting for that, I have to look daily to the Lord for His wisdom in order to write what He desires. This isn't an easy process, but I've found that it has worked wonderfully in past writing projects.

Waiting for the Lord to work in your situation will give you confidence and patience, removing fear and panic. As you allow His plan to unfold in your life, you'll realize that "He makes all things beautiful in His time." That's not your time but His time!

David, the psalmist, talked about his experiences of waiting before the Lord. In Psalm 40:1-3 he said, "I waited patiently for the Lord, and He inclined to me, and heard my cry. He also brought me up out of a horrible pit, out of the miry clay, and set my feet upon a rock, and established my steps. He has put a new song in my mouth—praise to our God; many will see it and fear, and will trust in the Lord."

That's something worth waiting for! God watches for our patience, then responds with His direction. Getting your feet planted on the rock beats living in the swamp. Carefully planting each step is far different than stumbling over your own feet. Singing a new song is a whole lot better than singing your old tune off-key.

It all starts with waiting—not just looking for God to make things happen, but for God Himself to happen in your life.

The second area involves waiting for God's healing process to bind up your wounds. I meet many people who've accumulated an assortment of wounds. You can't escape hurt if you're living in the real world. Our tendency in dealing with wounds is to want instant healing. We get this attitude largely from television and media advertisements. We expect a "plop, plop, fizz, fizz, oh what a relief it is!" response to both stomach upsets and emotional wounds. When that doesn't happen, we become impatient and discouraged with the recovery process and often try to ignore the pain.

It takes years for the hurts of divorce to heal. The things people say and the embarrassment you feel can make the healing process long and difficult.

When we learn to wait before the Lord, we also learn to wait for His healing touch according to His timetable. God *does* want our hurts to be healed. His concern for all healing in our lives is revealed in Exodus 15:26: "If you diligently heed the voice of the Lord your God and do what is right in His sight, give ear to His commandments and keep all His statutes, I will put none of the diseases on you which I have brought on the Egyptians. For I am the Lord who heals you." You'll notice that healing comes from listening to the voice of the Lord. Listening demands waiting. Many hurts go unresolved because we aren't willing to collect them, bring them before the Lord, and wait for what He will say to us about them.

Sometimes God walks us through pain again in order to effect healing. Sometimes we are simply and miraculously released from it. God understands best the process that will aid our growth.

Waiting for healing in the emotional and spiritual realm requires patience. But it's far better than trying to run through life with your wounds still bleeding! How is your healing process going?

The third area is waiting for other people. Have you ever prepared a wonderful dinner, only to have your guests appear an hour late? Have you ever arrived late to a concert because you had to wait for friends who are never on time? Waiting for others is as difficult for most of us as waiting in line.

We wait for others to become as mature and wise as we are. We wait for them to "grow up" or "get their act together." When that doesn't happen in 60 seconds, we often become impatient and move on to other people.

I stress to post-divorce people the importance of building some relationships with others who are on the same growth level. A second marriage between a person divorced one year, and someone divorced seven years can be problematic. I don't suggest that the person divorced seven years wait for five or six years until the other person catches up. The best wisdom might be to look for someone who is closer to where you are in life. This also holds true for men and women who are widowed, since many widowed people marry divorced people.

One of the tougher areas related to waiting for others involves children. We want them to grow up; but even more, we want them to understand where we are and where we've come from. The struggle is that parents and children don't want to wait on one another. Adjusting to the loss of a parent through death or divorce is as hard on a child as it is on the adult.

Waiting for others also demands understanding and approval. Many divorced people desperately want others to understand their struggle and to say they love and accept them. Losing the affirmation of others is often devastating after a divorce. Too many people imply they really don't care to understand what you've gone through or what you might still be facing. If you are waiting for your church to accept your divorce and love you in spite of it, you could wait a long time. The church is slowly discovering that divorced people have a right to keep on living without constant judgment, indictment, and condemnation. Similarly, widowed people should be able to live without loneliness, rejection, and abandonment.

The fourth type of waiting is waiting for yourself. It's one thing to wait on things outside yourself. It's quite another to wait on things within. It is easy to become enslaved to the "Why did I do that?" mentality. From that point, it's easy to put yourself down and not get up too often.

Most of us are slow growers. We've all seen the sign saying, "Please be patient—God isn't finished with me yet." Perhaps it should say, "I must be patient with myself—God isn't finished with me yet."

We can all get down on ourselves. Elijah, after one of the greatest victories in the Bible, ended up crying the blues under a bush.

Being patient with yourself is directly related to waiting on the Lord. If the Lord is working in you, the promise of Philippians 1:6 will become reality, "Being confident of this very thing, that He who has begun a good work in you will complete it until the day of Jesus Christ."

Don't be so restless with yourself that you deny God's gentle, patient guiding in your life. When we absorb God's patient example, we will learn how to wait on the human and imperfect parts of ourselves. God does His work slowly and thoroughly. Being patient allows Him that freedom.

Often people will be impatient with you as you wait upon the Lord and on yourself. Let that be their problem, not yours. Your greatest danger is pushing the river rather than going with the flow of it. Psalm 37:7 says, "Rest in the Lord and wait patiently for Him." I can wait on myself if I know I'm waiting on the Lord.

The fifth area of waiting is for God's timing or His openings. Too few of us really wait for God to open the doors He wants us to walk through. We are in the habit of opening our own doors and asking God's blessing as we stride through them. Consequently, we run into a lot of dead ends and wonder why. The shortest distance between two doorways in life is measured by God's yardstick, not ours.

As I grow older, I've discovered that I want to speedily open the doors that remain in my life. Perhaps you have the same problem. It's a good thing that age doesn't mean a whole lot to God. He certainly is never in a hurry! God spends a lot of time directing us toward where He wants us to go.

Solomon understood the concept of waiting on God when he admonished, "In all your ways acknowledge Him, and He shall direct your paths"

(Prov. 3:6). This simply means asking God for direction and allowing Him to point out the road or door. It takes a mature, sensitive Christian, when faced with making a decision, to say he or she is waiting for the Lord to open the right door, whether for a job change, a move to a new town or state, a career change, or a relationship change. How great it is to know that God is leading you in a specific way, and to share that knowledge with others! How exciting to realize that God has told you to do something but hasn't yet revealed how He will bring it about!

I believe that God gives us little challenges to trust Him with before He gives us big ones. When He knows we're waiting and listening, He isn't hesitant to speak.

A sixth area of waiting is for a special someone to marry and enjoy, happily ever after. Living in the relational waiting room of life can grind down your endurance, destroying the faith you once had that there is always someone for everyone.

Some Reasons Why That Special Person Hasn't Appeared

The first is that God knows you are not ready for the relationship. You may feel ready, think you're ready, and act ready, but God is saying, "Not yet." Again, waiting for the Lord's timing in this area is tough.

The second reason is that the special person God intends for you isn't ready yet. I know you'd like to know who it is so you can help speed up the process! Let God take control. He knows more about the person than you do.

The third reason could be that your situation or theirs needs to change before either of you will be ready for a relationship. This means your preparation process isn't finished yet, nor is that special someone's.

A fourth reason is that you need more time to grow and build your own life. Most of us are slow learners and we think we're ready for many things long before their time. Many second marriages fail because they're not ready and it's too soon.

It certainly isn't easy, but I encourage you to pray for patience and a deeper understanding of God's timing in this area of your life.

Waiting has always been part of God's plan for us. Watching the seasons of the year change, your children grow up, and seeing the sunrise are all part of God's waiting process.

God calls us to be more patient. We'll get things done a whole lot better, and perhaps even a bit faster if we begin by waiting on Him. How much waiting on God have you done lately?

Assessing Personal Growth

1. Are you a good "wait-er"? Why or why not?
2. Describe ways you've learned to wait on the Lord.
3. Do you become impatient waiting for those around you to "grow up"? Why?
4. Are you often impatient with yourself? How does that affect you?
5. What doors are you most eager to have opened in your life?
6. Finish this statement: In the area of learning to wait, I need to _____.

Chapter
Fourteen

Forgiveness: God's Detergent

*"Forgiveness is surrendering my right to hurt you back
if you hurt me."*

Dr. Archibald Hart

Wendy rose to leave my office. With tears running down her cheeks, she looked at me and said, "How can I ever forgive myself for what I've done? I feel so guilty!" I've lost track of how many times I've heard similar expressions from single-again people. Most of them are specific about the situations that bind them with guilt. Some fear there is no release from the guilt of a failed marriage. For a few singles, it becomes a haunting feeling they are never able to resolve.

The usual route to guilt goes something like this. You start thinking about a situation that happened in the past. You reflect on its negative outcome in your life and wonder what things would be like now if your response had been different. The "If I'd only" game comes into focus, its thoughts taking over your mind. As you begin to get buried in yesterday's memories, you start to feel guilty. You wish you could either change it all, or forget it forever.

Life is a series of choices, and all of us make bad ones at some time. We choose the wrong mate, move to the wrong city, go to the wrong college, pursue the wrong vocation, and end up feeling guilty about our choices. Remember, though, we have the freedom to fail! If that freedom is to be part

121

of our growth, we can't afford to feel guilty when we're unsuccessful. The failure or the wrong decision should become a teaching experience, not a guilt box that closes us off from further development.

Guilt in Divorce

There are three primary areas of guilt associated with the divorce process. In talking with thousands of people in divorce-recovery workshops, these three areas always come up.

1. Inadequacies. When things go wrong, we jump on the teeter-totter of *blame.* We tip the balance one way and place all the blame for what happened on the other person. Then we tip the balance the other way and assume all the blame ourselves. This inevitably results in a martyr complex, a self-pity syndrome, and a great bout of depression. Doing this makes us look good and all the world look wrong.

Author John Powell says, "Blaming is a game. It removes me from reality. Blaming is essentially a way of shifting responsibility and maintaining power over others. Growth begins where blaming ends."

You must avoid the "blame game" and deal with your inadequacies. That means simply being honest enough with yourself to admit you don't have all the answers. No one is adequate in every situation. I meet many people who feel as if reading one more self-improvement book will make them adequate in every area of life. This is simply not going to happen. Accepting your inadequacies is acknowledging your humanity. God didn't create you to be a robot or a computer. You are a person, with human strengths and weaknesses.

I listen to long lists of inadequacies that people share with me as they go through a divorce. They feel they're inadequate in love, parenting, personality, patience, understanding, wisdom, empathy, kindness, ambition, sensitivity, and so on. Your list might be a lot longer. After you name them all, ask yourself, "So what?" Are you going to merely admit to them, then hide behind them as an excuse not to deal with life? Or are you ready to tackle some of those areas you need help with? A healthy response would be to shout out loud, "I blew it!" and then get on with the rest of your life, learning how not to blow it as badly in the future.

2. Indecision. I meet many single-again people who have a terrible time making up their minds. Their future is often on hold because they can't decide what to do. Some blame even their divorce on their indecision.

At times, we are all indecisive. We don't want to make the wrong choice, so we often avoid making any choices at all.

Yesterday's indecision can prohibit you from making the choices you need to make today. You mustn't indict yourself for lacking resolution in the past. The words "If I'd only" are dangerous and ineffective—they can't change yesterday's mistakes. If your nature is still to be indecisive, I would suggest you get some help from a counselor or friend.

One of the most common indecisions I hear from divorced people is, "I wish we would've made up our minds to go to a counselor or marriage specialist in time to prevent this divorce." However, hindsight is valuable only as a teacher for today and tomorrow.

Indecision can cause guilt from which there is no release. It can keep your mind in reverse, seldom allowing you to deal with today's decisions. Forget the decisions you wish you had made. Get on with the ones you can make right now.

3. Decisions. When was the last time you made a hasty decision and later regretted it? You stand in the movie ticket line that seems to be moving the fastest, and it stalls. The other lines sail by you, and you continue to wait. Wrong decision! You move into what seems to be the faster moving lane on the highway, only to find yourself in a traffic jam. Wrong decision!

Life can fill up pretty quickly with wrong decisions that are much more serious than those. Too many of these bad choices can send you running and create enormous guilt.

When you go through a divorce, you are reminded of the decision you made to get married. Now that you are at the point of divorce, it seems you made the wrong choice. As you look around at people who are still married, it seems as though they made the right decision. You are wrong, they are right, and the guilt begins to sweep over you.

All of us make some decisions based on too little information, and too much emotion. We can't undo them, or run from them. But we can learn from past mistakes and move on with our lives.

Guilt over Death

Stephanie approached, thanking me for the memorial service I had just conducted. As she was about to walk away, she said, "If I had only made John take better care of himself, he would be alive today!" Her feelings, if entertained for long, could bring about a deep sense of guilt over her husband's death. Many people who lose a mate by death feel they could have done something to prevent it from happening. Guilt feelings about not doing certain things can cling to a person for a long time.

It seems there's no place to deal with the guilt that arises after a death. It's so final that you can't even offer an apology for what you felt you did wrong. The best resolution is to realize you did the best you knew how. Again, hindsight is valuable only when you use it to light the pathway ahead.

Anger is another emotion people often feel after their mate dies. One man said to me, "How could my wife just go and die, leaving me with four children? I'm so angry at her for leaving me with all this responsibility." The waves of emotion about being left alone are difficult to calm. Each day, the aloneness increases the anger. Guilt about feeling angry only adds to the confusion.

Express your feelings honestly and talk them out with trusted friends. You will begin to find relief and be able to turn your focus from what used to be to what is.

The Way Out of Guilt

One of the best tools God has given us to handle guilt is forgiveness. Guilt always adds to more guilt. Forgiveness, however, sets us free from guilt.

I was about six years old when I decided to become a cookie thief. Mom had just baked some of her chocolate-chip specials. I was going through the kitchen and out to play when I decided to snatch a few without Mom's permission. About an hour later, she called me in from play and asked if I had taken any cookies. After a thorough grilling by my mother, I admitted to the theft. (It was pretty obvious, since I was the only other person at home.) Mom sent me to my room for the next two hours as punishment—a grueling sentence in the days when a boy's bedroom was not a haven full of entertaining electronic equipment.

After two hours of boredom, Mom released me. But a strange thing happened. I had served my time, but I wasn't sure I was really forgiven. I hung around the house pouting until Mom patted me on the head and assured me everything was all right and I could go outside to play. Those pats on the head were what I needed. They meant I was *really* forgiven, and any guilt I still felt was removed. I was free to move on with my life without a permanent blot on my record.

Forgiveness is God's detergent to make us clean again. In 1 John 1:9, we see the heart of God embodied in the forgiveness process. It says, "If we confess our sins, He is faithful and just, and will forgive our sins and cleanse us from all unrighteousness."

Confession brings wonderful cleansing and forgiveness. It's an admission of our inability to do everything right. We admit our humanity, our weakness, our imperfection. We recognize wrong decisions, indecision, anger, and guilt.

Confession is saying, "I blew it and I'm sorry." It is taking the blame ourselves.

Accepting God's promise of forgiveness means that I must forgive others as well. It was Peter who asked Jesus how many times we should forgive another person. Peter asked if seven times was enough. Jesus' response was 70 times seven. What He really meant wasn't 490 times, but an unlimited number of times.

I'm sure many men and women would like to do their weekly laundry just once and have it clean for the rest of their lives. The problem is that the clothes we wear get dirty and need to be washed. It's a never-ending chore.

In a way, we are like that laundry pile. We get pretty scruffy from life. We need a constant application of God's finest detergent—forgiveness! If you need to ask God's forgiveness, you might pray something like this:

> God, forgive me for the things I feel guilty about not doing. Forgive me for the things I feel guilty about doing. I confess to You my inadequacies and accept Your continuous promise of forgiveness. Amen.

Recently I spoke to a large group of singles about forgiveness. During the question period, a woman asked to share a few thoughts from her own experience regarding forgiveness.

She told us she and her ex-spouse were bitter enemies and had spoken little since their divorce. She had struggled with not being able to ask him for forgiveness. Finally, she took the risk, went to him, and asked him to forgive her for the things she knowingly and unknowingly had done wrong that had contributed to their marriage failure. He forgave her and also asked the same of her. She told us, "It seemed as though all the hate, hurt, anger, and guilt just evaporated the moment we forgave. I have never felt better and more relieved of a burden in my whole life. Forgiveness works!"

In my desk, I have a file of letters that contain similar accounts. Forgiveness is really God's ultimate guilt remover! It sets us free to go on with our lives. It releases us from having to try to be perfect and lets us simply be human. It settles accounts with other people who often load us with guilt.

Jesus personified ultimate forgiveness on the cross when He uttered the words, "Father, forgive them; for they know not what they do" (Luke 23:34). Sometimes we don't really know what we are doing, either. We need God's forgiveness, and the forgiveness of others. When we learn to exercise God's provision of forgiveness, we will be guilt-free!

During my travels recently, someone handed me the following clipping. Regretfully, there was no source to credit.

1. Forgiveness is a decision, not a feeling.
2. Forgiveness is showing mercy even when the injury has been deliberate.
3. Forgiveness is accepting the person as he or she is.
4. Forgiveness is taking a risk . . . it is making myself vulnerable.
5. Forgiveness is accepting an apology.
6. Forgiveness is choosing to love.

Assessing Personal Growth

1. How do you usually handle things that make you feel guilty?
2. How much guilt are you assuming for your present single-again status?
3. Describe an experience in which your guilt disappeared when you asked for forgiveness.
4. Are you living with an experience for which you desire forgiveness but don't feel you have it?
5. How easy or difficult is it for you to forgive another person?

Chapter Fifteen

The Possibility
of Reconciliation

"God is bigger than our blunders and not immobilized by our sins."
William Hulme

G od's going to put my marriage back together," Deanne exclaimed, as
she hurried out the door after our divorce support group ended. I
caught up with her and asked, "Tell me more."

As she began to elaborate, I realized I was listening to a story I'd heard
hundreds of times in my years of counseling and teaching. Deanne had
listened to an estranged couple tell their incredible story of reconciliation
after a two-year separation. As she watched their account on a Christian television show, she heard both the man and woman say, as they looked directly
into the television camera, "What God has done for us He can do for anyone
hearing our story today."

Before the program had even concluded, Deanne was on the road to
reconciliation in her mind. It mattered little that her former spouse was about
to remarry someone else in a few weeks. She had grabbed the thread of hope
the television couple had tossed her way, and was hanging on for dear life. I
wondered what would happen to her and her belief system if reconciliation
with her spouse did not happen.

One of the questions I've been most frequently asked as a counselor and teacher in the field of divorce recovery is, "Do you think there is any hope my husband and I (or wife and I) will get back together?" I wish I could tell all of them, "Yes, definitely!" In all honesty, though, my experience has been that very few couples reconcile and continue their journey through marriage. Before I surround you with dark clouds of doom, let me say that I am a hopeful person, but I have learned to keep my hope plugged into reality.

Twenty years ago, in my book *Growing Through Divorce*, I said there is hope for reconciliation when any two people will work together with a professional counselor over a long period of time. When only one person is willing to do that, chances of restoration are slim to none. The tragedy is that it takes two people to get married but only one to get divorced. If one person wants the marriage to work and the other does not, a reunion will be close to impossible.

The Pressures

If you're a Christian, your entire belief system is put on the line when you get caught in the throes of divorce. On the one hand, you know God hates divorce even more than you do—but your marriage seems headed for divorce country anyway. On the other hand, pressure from Christian friends and the church community mandates that you stop the divorce from happening. You're told to pray, have more faith, and take a firm stand against the devil and his forces. Along with this tide of pressure usually come your children, who implore you to somehow stop the divorce from ruining their lives.

As the divorce process gathers speed, even God seems unable to stop it and you begin to question everything you believe and have been taught about God's power, miracles, answered prayer, and faith. In lucid moments, your throbbing question is, "How do you prevent something you don't want to happen from occurring, especially if you are a Christian?" Sadly, the answer is that you often cannot stop it, in spite of what others might say.

Today, in the world of divorcing Christians (or even divorcing non-Christians), about 75 percent are men and women who have been left for another person. The remaining 25 percent are those who chose to leave a dysfunctional relationship in order to survive and stay alive. Usually, the second group does not want a reconciliation unless their spouse is willing to receive help. Tragically, however, many dysfunctional spouses refuse help, and divorce becomes a reality. For the larger group who have been left for another person, their "about to be former spouse" tends to put energy into building the new relationship, rather than restoring their marriage. My years of experience have confirmed that once a third party gets involved in any way, the chance of reconciliation is remote. Third parties push their own agenda, not reconciliation with a former spouse.

The Realities

Reality is always hard to accept. Fantasy is much easier to deal with. No matter what you wish, and what others may wish for you, *some marriages cannot and will not be put back together*. I have tried desperately to help put the marriages of some of my friends back together, only to realize failure in spite of all my knowledge, love, prayers, and concern. It was hard for me to accept. Like many others, I walked away asking myself, "How could this happen? Why did this happen?" Even years after these divorces, the reality is still hard to assimilate into my life.

One of the toughest realities to accept is that no matter how hard you begged, pleaded, cried, promised, and yelled at God, He did not intervene in any miraculous or ordinary way to save your marriage. I am sure God must struggle with the fact that He gave humans the right to choose, and some people make bad choices that others must live out, sometimes until they die. Many divorced men and women are living out the bad decision their spouse made to leave them and file for divorce. A spouse's bad decision can make your life miserable and difficult for a long time. It can also make the lives of your children a struggle, as they try to understand all the emotions and feelings of a home that has come apart.

A third reality is the realization that you missed the signals of a marriage in trouble months or years ago and failed to get help when needed. Many divorced people carry that guilt long after their divorce is finalized. They regularly beat themselves up and take all the blame. Even when told their spouse made a bad decision in leaving them, they want to assume all the responsibility by responding, "It's my fault. I must have done something wrong."

We can deal with guilt through the process of forgiveness, but it still takes time and hard work. Forgiving yourself is a difficult task, but it also can set you free to move ahead and grow.

A fourth reality is dealing with the belief that "Christians don't get divorced!" Those who toss that unnerving phrase at you never stop long enough to ask what happened and how they can help you recover. Their tendency is to judge, indict, convict, and sentence before you can run and hide in the church restroom. Advice-givers fail to realize there are some things neither you nor God can fix without the willingness of the other person (your former spouse).

Many divorced men and women have fled the church because fellow Christians lack love and understanding. There's a familiar saying that "the Christian army tends to shoot its wounded." It's true that many divorced men and women have become the walking wounded.

What You Can't Do

You can't make someone love you. Remember when you were a teenager and your steady broke up with you? He or she wanted to move on and you didn't. You probably worked day and night to find ways to get the person back, only to realize it was fruitless and that you needed to move on too. I've watched people act silly, even tragically, in order to revive a hopeless lost love.

Second, you can't make someone want to be with you when they don't want to. Many separated and divorced people have said, "If I can just find a way to be with them or around them, they will love me again and we will have a chance." Their futile attempts only end up in tragic rejection and more pain.

Third, you can't make God do things. God gives orders; He doesn't take them. He lets people have the freedom to choose, and is willing to wait to intervene until they come to Him in submission.

Fourth, you can't blame everyone else for your circumstances. You are responsible for yourself and your situation. Blame is a game that keeps you from personal growth and self-responsibility.

Finally, you can't put your life on hold forever, waiting for a former spouse to come back to you. When it's time for closure, you must move on with your life and pursue personal growth.

What You Can Do

Now you're probably thinking, "Wow! This guy sure doesn't offer a person much hope." Well, after 20 years of working in divorce country, I've found there are some things you can do if you want your marriage restored. Please realize, I'm offering you wisdom, not guarantees.

1. You can set up a time frame to wait, watch, and pray for guidance. Some spouses who leave need time to realize they've made a mistake. Unless they are already remarried, you can keep a window open to see if they will want to reconcile. Often we are in too great a hurry and our haste limits God's ability to work in the life of another person. While you are waiting and praying, watch what's happening. Is the behavior of your former spouse dismissing all hope of reconciliation? Can you see tangible ways God is working in their life? Watch what is happening, not what you wish was happening.

2. Get some counseling for yourself and know that it's for YOU. This can help you build a game plan for your life and help you stay accountable. It can guide you in areas of personal growth, as well as help you unload emotional baggage you may have been carrying for years.

3. You can try to get your former spouse in counseling with you. This is hard to do if your spouse feels you were the problem or if he or she is already involved with another person. Remember, you can't make someone do something they don't want to do.

4. Look for resource people who can help you build possible reconciliation bridges. Relatives, friends, and pastors can be good resources. Remember, God can use other people you may not even know to help you.

5. Find a divorce support group to join. Kindred spirits can lend help and guidance to your daily struggle. I have seen some genuine miracles happen in support groups over the years. A support group will also keep you honest in what you see, feel, and experience.

6. Practice forgiveness in your life. We all build walls that isolate us from one another. Forgiveness is one method that brings those barriers down.

7. Don't put your life in neutral and live on hold. Do things that will help you move ahead. Going back to school, finding a new career, making new friends all will promote growth. Don't say, "I better not do that in case my ex-spouse and I get back together." Any reconciliation can always make room for the new things in your life.

8. Ask God the question, "God, what do You want me to do?" Listen for His answer each day. With God's help, be willing to examine your own spiritual life and make wrong things right with God.

9. Realize that if a reconciliation does happen, it may be months or even years down the road. God works in a different time frame than we do. Reconciliation means change, and most of us don't handle change easily. Any reconciliation that doesn't involve drastic change is a hollow one at best.

10. Realize when you hear other people's stories that they are OTHER people's stories. God is not in the photocopying business. You can celebrate another's story and victory, but it is original to that person; it is not reproducible.

Do I believe reconciliation is possible? Yes! Do I believe it will happen for everyone? No! Do I believe God loves you even if you never have a reconciliation? Yes! Yes! Yes!

Assessing Personal Growth

1. Do you feel there is any possibility for a reconciliation with your former spouse? Why? Why not?

2. What things need to happen to make that a possibility for you?

3. What things need to happen to make that a possibility for your spouse?

4. How do you handle living without the possibility of reconciliation?

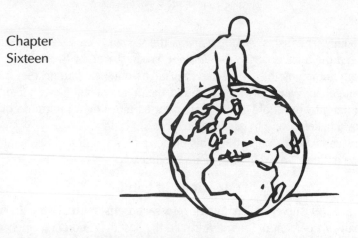

Chapter
Sixteen

We Are Still a Family

Train up a child in the way he should go,
and when he is old he will not depart from it.

Prov. 22:6

N o fun vacation for us this year! We're just not a family anymore!" Janet
said, at our weekly divorce support group.

I've listened to thousands of similar responses from single parents
when I've asked about future plans. Janet's answer especially haunted me as I
drove home. "We're just not a family anymore!"

If divorce is the dissolution of a marriage, does it also mean the death of a
family? If a mother or father dies suddenly, does a family cease to exist? Does
the only hope for family rebirth lie in remarriage?

For many single parents, the dream of an all-American family slips over
the horizon when the sun sets in divorce country or at a local memorial
garden. Family love and togetherness are replaced by the stark realities of too
little money with too many bills, too little time with too many needs, and too
little energy with too many problems. The crush of daily demand and harried
schedules seems to leave little quality time for family fun, warmth, and
emotional closeness.

Author and researcher Robert Weiss sums up the state of single parent
pressures today by suggesting three major tasks that are necessary to run any

133

basic family. The first is *making a living*, the second is *maintaining the household*, and the third is *caring for children*. When shared by two parents, those tasks are not impossible. But when they fall on only one parent, they become mind-boggling. Weiss further states that the dream of still being a family in a single parent household is often abandoned more by a multitude of tasks than by a belief system in family gone awry.

How can a single parent and his or her children still feel like a family in the face of these overwhelming responsibilities?

Four Kinds of Family

In a 1989 survey taken by the Massachusetts Mutual Life Insurance Company, 74 percent of those asked said the best definition of a family was "a group of people who love and care for each other." My dictionary defines family as "a group of parents and their children" (apparently no love and care needed). Another recent definition cited family as "a group of adults sharing a common household." How would you define a family?

Whatever your answer, the word *family* today includes:

1. The family into which you were born. You had no choice about this. Your family of origin was your introduction to people on this earth. From them you were either given support and love or denied it.

2. The family into which you marry. Most adults join this kind of family at some point in their lives. Soon children begin arriving. Within this family grow new goals and new dreams. But sometimes, divorce or death shatters them. In the blink of an eye, everything changes.

3. The single-parent family. As we are all aware, this is a fast-growing group that now comprises nearly 30 percent of our nation's families with children under 18. In fact, a 12 percent increase of single-parent families is expected by the year 2000.

Everyone, of course, is familiar with these three models of family in today's culture. There is, however, a fourth kind of family that can be integrated into all the above.

4. The family of God. The individual who has accepted Jesus Christ as Lord and Savior joins a new family. Scripture verifies this in Ephesians 2:19, "Consequently, you are no longer foreigners and aliens, but fellow citizens with God's people and members of God's household." Our decision to follow Jesus makes all the other members of His family our brothers and sisters in

Christ. Your family of origin can die out and leave you alone. You can lose the family you married into through death or divorce. But you will never be without a family when you are a member of God's household! No matter what has happened in your past, your future is bright.

Author C. S. Lewis once said there are three statements that firmly connect all hurting people to each other. You may have said them recently: "What! You too? I thought I was the only one." Knowing you are not alone and being able to share your needs with other members of God's family can help immeasurably in the single-parent home. And it can give you the conviction to go back home with this positive message—We're still a family!

Ten Ways to Build a Stronger Family Awareness

As head of your house, you can build up your family through these actions:

1. Remind your children each day that you are still a family. Use the word *family* often.

2. Plan fun outings where each member of the family can share in all aspects. Learn to laugh and play together. Remember, there are many free things a family can do together. To name a few, bike-riding, flying kites, rollerblading, and visiting museums and libraries.

3. Structure your family's spiritual growth. A devotional time in which each family member is free to contribute is important. You also might attend Christian concerts, watch Christian videos, and build a spiritual library. Don't rely solely on your church for your family's spiritual growth. It is the responsibility of every family member, with the single parent leading the way.

4. Support other family members at school, sports, and church events. Become each others' cheerleaders!

5. Live as close as possible to primary family members. Supportive grandparents or other extended family members can keep family connectedness alive.

6. Retain cherished family traditions and create new ones that all members can share in. Many single parents drop established family events because they are associated with a person who is no longer present. If traditions cannot be continued, replace them with others that are equally significant.

7. Join a single-parent fellowship group at your church or in your community. If none is available, start one and invite other single-parent families. These groups give both parents and children a sense of identity, community, and family through their common values, vision, and understanding.

8. Share activities with other single-parent families as well as with two-parent families so your children can see how others function. Many single parents surrender their children to child care services at every opportunity so they can be alone with other single adults. This hinders the family concept and causes emotional and social isolation between parents and children.

9. Plan family fund-raising projects that allow each member to contribute toward a goal such as a camping trip, vacation, new trail bikes, etc.

10. Buy scrapbooks and picture albums for this new chapter in your family's activities and celebrations. Many single-parent families fail to do this and end up with no tangible record of these years.

Don'ts for Single-Parent Families

1. Don't let your family members become "lone rangers" who consistently go their own way and do their own thing. Spend time together. Make each member accountable for his or her actions and decisions.

2. Don't call your family a "broken home."

3. Don't stay away from single- or two-parent family activities because of the guilt or shame you might feel about your situation.

4. Don't throw "pity parties" for your family, blaming all your present woes and problems on your former spouse, your family of origin, or Murphy's Law.

5. Don't allow daily and weekly schedules to become so crowded that you have no quality time for family togetherness and warmth.

6. Decide today that every problem and struggle you have as a single parent is merely another mountain to climb with the help of God. "'For I know the plans I have for you,' declares the Lord, 'plans to prosper you and not to harm you, plans to give you hope and a future'" (Jer. 29:11).

Remember Janet at the beginning of this chapter? I later asked her why there were no family vacation plans in her summer. She replied that her former spouse had always planned the vacations, and she could never do it on her own with four children.

After several weeks of encouragement from her friends, Janet relented and tackled the plans for a 10-day vacation with her children. When August rolled around, they headed for Disneyland, Sea World, and the San Diego Zoo.

The next time I saw her, she was ecstatic. The whole family proclaimed they'd had the best vacation ever! Her final word to me, "We are still family and will continue to do what families do!"

What can you do to proclaim to the world, but most of all to those living in your house, that you are still a family?

Chapter Seventeen

Being Me
and Growing Free

"Change is inevitable, but growth is intentional."

Many suddenly single-again people choose to live at the point of their death or divorce crisis for far too long. A crisis impedes growth. It provides an excuse for those who want to hide and avoid new beginnings. It becomes a convenient cocoon in which to harbor the past and hinder the future.

Life goes on, and you must go on as well. You can break free of a crisis when you're willing to enter life's emergency room and begin treatment. The mourning and grieving come to an end when you are willing to start new growth.

Repairing Your Wounds

If I put my hand through a window and received a six-inch cut, would I race off to the local hospital and book myself a room for the next six months? No! I would go to the emergency room and ask if I could have my wound stitched up. Generally, in the space of an hour or so, my wound would be bandaged; I would be free to return home, ready to repair the window I'd just broken. My progress would be impaired, and I might even have some pain, but I'd go about my day and my tasks just as before.

Receiving help is always a part of the healing process. Many people are simply too proud or too scared to ask for someone to help heal their hurts. But there are caring people who will give their hands and hearts when someone goes through a divorce or death crisis.

As the initial pain subsides, new pains come along. Loneliness, fear of the future, self-doubt, loss of friends, and indecision are some. It's important to find others who will help you through the whole process of mending the extra cuts and bruises that appear along the way.

The beginning of a new life is a frightening experience. Several people have shared with me that their divorce was like an operation. It took a while to recover from the surgery, and they felt as if they were taking weekly trips to the hospital for further repairs. There seemed to be so many things the surgery failed to resolve. Some of those repairs addressed inner healing of the spirit, while others involved the practical, everyday human needs we all have. Many single-again people feel they should simply get well all of a sudden and never need minor repairs again.

A newly divorced man told me he was going to have a T-shirt printed up with the slogan, "Temporarily out of commission." He wanted to wear it on the days when things were rocky and he needed some outside help in his life.

Do you feel free enough to go to the emergency room once in a while for some stitching up? Maybe it's just an emotional lift you need, a solid word of encouragement, an affirmation, an idea. Other times it may mean going to a professional counselor or therapist. These "visits" don't mean you are doing poorly. They mean that you are choosing to do better. Don't be afraid to ask for help as your new journey unfolds.

Meeting Your Needs

As I've talked and counseled with countless numbers of single-again people, they've shared five basic needs. These needs become the basis for solid growth in single living. As I share them, do a mental checkup on yourself and see how you're doing.

Relational needs. In an earlier chapter I talked about building relationships. I dealt with the personal side, the one-to-one relationships we all need. Along with the personal, we need a supportive group of friends who form a community for us. Because many single-again people lose their married community support systems, it's important to build a new system that will add meaning and continuity to life. One of the fastest growing ministries in churches across America is directed towards single adults. Many churches have over 500 singles in their programs.

The church-oriented singles community provides an ideal place for single-again people to meet new friends and build strong relationships. The church group also offers an alternative to some of the secular singles groups known for their "search and seizure" agendas.

Single-again people quickly discover that it's no fun doing things alone. A singles group provides the opportunity to do things with a community. It also brings support when you are struggling with new beginnings. If you're in a singles group, you are not alone; the people in it are fellow strugglers.

Most people do two things with group experiences: they choose to either isolate themselves from the group, or they relate to it. Those in isolation seldom grow and often are buried in loneliness and self-pity. People who reach out find community and caring, and are also able to provide that support for others. It's comforting to know that others have problems too. Mutual strength and support come from shared lives.

I get letters from many singles who ask how to find a singles group in their area. Few singles find a group to join on their first attempt. Usually you have to visit several groups before you find one you feel comfortable in. You can determine the quality of a group by observing the following things:

1. Lots of laughing, hugging, and a general warm spirit.
2. A well-planned and executed program.
3. A friendly welcome to first-time attendees.
4. Literature telling about upcoming events.
5. A good mix of both men and women in the group.
6. The people directing the program are alive and sparkling.
7. You get a call or letter after your visit asking how you liked the meeting and inviting you to the next function.

Don't get discouraged in your search for a good singles community. Take the time to make your rounds. It can be as important to your life as finding a good dentist, doctor, or car mechanic.

Another word of caution—you can become worn out in a group. Being overworked and scarcely thanked in positions of responsibility can send you running for cover. You may need to take it easy once in a while and rest in the back row while the group ministers to you. Always give your group a chance to love you. Then you can truly love them in return.

Social needs. When you ask single people how their social life is, they might respond by saying they aren't dating anyone right now. Dating is a part of your social existence, but it doesn't mean your life is the pits because you lack that special someone. I define social life as the fun things I do with other people. Married people tend to do social things with each other or with other married friends. Many single-again people allow their social lives to fall into ruin because they can't envision themselves having fun with anyone other than the people they once associated with.

Building a social existence as a newly single person involves trying some things you've never done before. New social adventures can put excitement back into your life. Make a list of some of the things you would like to try: skydiving, learning to fly, skiing, taking music lessons, rafting on the river, hiking in the wilderness. Don't be stopped by thinking, "I've never done that before."

I vividly remember Clara, the quiet little lady in one of our singles groups who was always organizing backpacking trips. She was well over 60, and more feminine than muscular. Yet she was the first to shoulder her backpack and head out on the trail each morning. When everyone else was dying of exhaustion, Clara was over the rim of the next hill. It was an entirely new hobby she took up after her husband died.

Discovering new hobbies you can share with others in your singles group will help you grow socially.

Spiritual needs. In the course of counseling appointments, I sometimes ask single people how they are doing spiritually. Some respond by telling me they go to church, read their Bible occasionally, pray for their food before meals, and once in a while even tell somebody what they believe about God. For many, that appears to be the spiritual growth checklist. If they are doing all of them, they must be growing. The truth is, however, that they simply might be following mechanical rituals that have no effect on the inside.

Spiritual growth is building a relationship with God. It's being sensitive to what He would want in our lives. It is getting directions from God for daily decisions. This kind of growth takes time and often is not open for public inspection. It involves the same process we go through in building relationships with other human beings. Spiritual growth is walking with God through all the situations of life, believing His promises, and knowing that He loves us.

We relate to God on a one-to-one basis in our spiritual growth. We also connect with God through our Christian friends. They provide a spiritual climate and community of love in which our spiritual growth can thrive. Are you developing in your relationship with God? Do you have friends to mature with you? Do you belong to a church that enables you to grow?

Educational needs. Education can help you attain your fullest human potential. Many singles take academic courses in local colleges to further their careers and improve their salaries. On-the-job training programs are a part of continuing education. All this is important to building self-worth and self-esteem. But if it is the only educational program you have for yourself, you will fall short on the personal-growth level. Along with external growth, there must be something taking place on the inside of your life. Here is a list to reflect on as you consider doing some interior redesigning in your life.

1. How am I doing with expressing and handling my feelings and emotions?
2. Am I acting on situations in my life or reacting to them?
3. Am I learning to assert myself, or am I constantly being manipulated and intimidated?
4. Do I feel good about myself and believe that I am worth something as a person?
5. Am I making significant and important changes in my personality?
6. Do I have direction in my life, or am I letting others direct me?
7. Are my feelings of self-confidence growing? Do I increasingly believe in myself and my abilities?

That's a short list. You can probably add several more items after you get started.

There are many good self-help books that will assist your growth in any of these areas. Local schools offer courses designed to help you grow and become a more confident person. The opportunities are there for you. Don't sit numbly. Pick out the area you need help in and get it!

Emotional needs. In the past 20 years, I have watched many single-again people come to one of my groups for the first time. Some are so emotionally tired and overloaded with their problems that even their physical appearance is stooped. Conversing with them only verifies their emotional battles.

In divorce-recovery seminars, I tell people that the divorce war is generally waged on two fronts: practical and emotional. For most people, the emotional is far more difficult than the practical.

First of all, your emotions tend to yo-yo. Just when you have one set of feelings lined up, something happens to send them reeling off in another direction. Feelings of love and hate toward a former spouse are a good example of this. Several months after a separation or divorce, you see your former spouse in a store. You don't know whether you should run over, embrace him and say how badly you've missed him, or whether you should mash him against the shelves with your shopping cart. At best, you have feelings of ambivalence.

Memories have a way of emotionally hooking you. Just when you think you've filed and cataloged them, a word or picture instantly brings them back, and you may be upset for the rest of the day.

Emotions cannot be denied. They have to be sorted out, expressed, and dealt with. When emotions are repressed, they often explode when you least expect, like a well-shaken bottle of soda. Some single adults suffer from emotional whiplash when they get hit from behind by emotional problems they thought were taken care of, but in reality were simply ignored.

You can do several positive things to resolve and rebuild your emotional stability.

1. Don't lock yourself away with your emotions. Find a few trusted friends to share them with. Emotions are tied to your feelings, and feelings are neither right nor wrong. They just are.
2. Find ways to express your emotions. Talking is one way. Writing, in the form of a journal or diary, is another. Thinking through your emotions in moments of quiet meditation and reflection is also healthy. Emotions have a way of piling up on each other. It's hard to sort them out when they become entangled.
3. Recognize where your emotions are right now. If you know where you are, you will know where to head. Having someone say you shouldn't feel the way you do won't resolve your feelings. It will just hang a cloud of guilt over you.
4. Make positive plans to help get your emotions under control. Maybe temporarily escaping your present situation for a time will give you a break. Try a few days away to gain perspective.

Our emotional wiring is ever present. We can either let our emotions run unchecked, out of control, or we can own them and decide to be responsible for them. We can either let situations direct our feelings, or we can take charge of the situations and our emotions. Growing up emotionally will help you feel good about yourself.

The Healing Goes On

In John 5:9, we read about the ending of one part of a man's life, and the beginning of another. The verse says, "At once the man recovered, picked up his bed and began to walk" (Phillips). This biblical account illustrates a man who was brought to the crossroads of a new beginning. His change of direction came through a healing miracle. Physically he became well. But that's only part of his story. The writer tells us the man "began to walk." That indicates that the second half of his healing was a process, not an event.

Divorce and death are not events. They are processes to walk through and live out. Healing for the man in John 5 involved a new direction—a learning process that could not be speeded up. Many single-again people are in a hurry to get on down the road. They look for the quickest and easiest answers to their struggles. Be aware that the quick answers are, at best, Band-Aids. They seldom address the heart of the matter.

All healing takes time. Beginning to walk means that a person might stumble and fall a bit, even slide backward. When small children take their first steps and fall midway across the three-foot distance to a parent's outstretched arms, they aren't spanked, placed in their crib, and told they will never be able to walk. They are promptly dusted off, placed with one parent, and shoved off again. This is repeated until children walk the distance. And it's not over when they walk the three feet. Then the distance is stretched to six feet, nine feet, and all the way across the room. Stumbling, falling, starting over . . . it's all a part of walking. Beginning to walk means

there will be good days and bad days
there will be setbacks and advances
there will be tears and laughter
there will be hurts and healings.

Right after the man in John 5 began his new journey, he was verbally attacked by those who couldn't affirm his healing and wanted to attack the healer. Sometimes when you are beginning to heal and get well, you make those around you nervous and jealous. Perhaps their growth isn't going as well as yours. Instead of asking for your help in their process, they become critical and envious of you. Don't let critical voices slow your healing. You may have to turn a deaf ear in their direction and continue on your course.

Healing life's hurts is a slow process. The greatest gift you can give yourself is the gift of time, After all, God is never in a hurry. His office hours are open for eternity.

Assessing Personal Growth

1. How do you feel your current relational needs are or aren't being met?
2. How has your social life changed since you became single again?
3. Describe how you feel you are doing in the area of emotional growth.
4. How far along do you feel you are in your healing process?
5. How do you feel when you go to singles functions where you've never attended before?

Appendix A

Children of divorce often end up like orphans of a violent war. They can be ignored by one parent or the other, shuttled between households, and left to wonder if they are living in a world where only adults have any rights.

The following "Bill of Rights" was created by some of our children's workers. We suggest you make copies of it to share with your own children. It will help them know they are loved and respected.

Children of Divorce
BILL OF RIGHTS

1. *The Right* to know that I am loved unconditionally.
2. *The Right* to know I didn't cause my parents' divorce.
3. *The Right* to know what caused the divorce.
4. *The Right* to have the security of knowing where I will live and with whom I will live.
5. *The Right* to be aware of how stress affects my life and how I can adapt to it in a healthy way.
6. *The Right* to be a kid and not be afraid of being myself.
7. *The Right* to have the guarantee that my physical and emotional needs will be met.
8. *The Right* not to be a victim of the past marriage and not to be used as a pawn between my parents.
9. *The Right* to have my own space for privacy to ensure respect for myself.
10. *The Right* to have a normal household routine and discipline to warrant a sense of security.
11. *The Right* to possess positive images of my parents so that I can love each parent equally.
12. *The Right* to have equal time and access with each parent.

Appendix B

Focus on the Family's
Statement on Divorce and Remarriage

Divorce represents one of the greatest failures in human life, and therefore one of the greatest heartbreaks. For this reason God hates divorce; it leaves abandoned dreams and broken promises where once there was hope.

Focus on the Family strongly opposes the idea that divorce constitutes a solution to marital discord or unhappiness, for often the problems of one marriage are carried to the next relationship. Jesus taught that in God's plan, marriage is meant for life.

Yet every marriage will at times be more of an ordeal than a love affair. The degree of commitment to God's principles and the confrontation of each partner's problems in these difficult times is what ultimately builds or destroys a marriage.

Focus on the Family is painfully aware that some marriages do fail and believes we must do all we can to care for the victims and their children. Dr. Dobson argues that it is extremely important not to become so caught up in expounding the biblical teachings on divorce (e.g., when it is permissible and when it is not) that we fail to show compassion for the individuals involved. The human heart is never served by condemnation. Focus on the Family sees itself particularly called to be an agent of healing and help in the midst of the tragedy of divorce, while still upholding the institution of marriage.

The issue of remarriage after divorce arouses even more controversy, and not all theologians agree. Focus on the Family holds that there are three sets of circumstances under which remarriage appears to be scripturally justified:

1. When the first marriage and divorce occurred prior to salvation. God's promise in 2 Corinthians 5:17—"If anyone is in Christ, he is a new creature; the old things have passed away; behold, new things have come"—applies to divorce as well as all other sins committed in the believer's past.

2. When one's mate is guilty of sexual immorality and is unwilling to repent and live faithfully with the marriage partner. However, we must be careful not to make Jesus' statement to this effect (Matthew 19:9) into a broad, sweeping, simplistic formula. Instead, we must evaluate each case independently, bearing in mind that "immorality" here refers to persistent, unrepentant behavior, and that divorce and remarriage is only an option for the faithful partner—not a command.

3. When an unbelieving mate willfully and permanently deserts a believing partner. This does not refer to a temporary departure, but to a permanent abandonment, where there is little or no hope of reviving former commitments and salvaging the relationship.

Notes

Chapter 4

1.Robert Weiss, *Loneliness: The Experience of Emotional and Social Isolation* (Cambridge, Mass.: M.I.T. Press, 1973).

Chapter 5

1.Lloyd Ahlem, *Do I Have to Be Me?* (Ventura, Calif.: Regal Books, 1973).

Chapter 6

1.Henri Nouwen, *The Wounded Healer* (New York: Doubleday, 1994).
2."Welcome Back" by Chuck Girard, copyright 1970, Dunamis Music, 8319 Lankershim Blvd., N. Hollywood, Calif. 91605. Used by permission. International copyright secured. All rights reserved.
3.Bruce Larson, *No Longer Strangers* (Waco, Tex.: Word Books, 1971).
4.John Powell, *Fully Human, Fully Alive* (Allen, Tex.: Tabor Pub., 1989).

Chapter 7

1.Maxwell Maltz, *Psycho-Cybernetics* (North Hollywood, Calif.: Wilshire, 1973).

Chapter 8

1."We All Get Hurt," by Dale Annis. Copyright 1975 by LEXICON MUSIC, INC. ASCAP. All rights reserved. International copyright secured. Used by special permission.

Resources

Other books and videos by Jim Smoke:

Growing Through Divorce, Harvest House Publishers

Growing In Remarriage, Fleming Revell Publishers

Facing Fifty: A View from the Mountaintop, Thomas Nelson Publishers

Moving Forward, A Divorce Recovery Devotional by Thomas Nelson Publishers

Forgiveness, A video by NSL, P.O. Box 1600, Grand Rapids, Michigan, 49501

Divorce: Surviving the Shock, A video by NSL, P.O. Box 1600, Grand Rapids, Michigan 49501

Other books:

Happiness is an Inside Job, by John Powell

Experiencing God, by Henry Blackaby and Claude King, Broadman Publishers

Lifemapping, by John Trent, Focus on the Family Publishing

To contact Jim Smoke personally: Jim Smoke
Grace Church
5100 Cerritos Ave.
Cypress, CA 90630

For further resources:

The National Association of Single Adult Leaders, P.O. Box 1600,Grand Rapids, Michigan 49501

Singles Ministry Resources, P.O. Box 60430, Colorado Springs, Colorado 80960

Single Parent Family Magazine, Focus on the Family, P.O. Box 35500, Colorado Springs, Colorado 80995

153